PREVENTING PRENATAL HARM

Clinical Medical Ethics

VOLUME 1

The titles published in this series are listed at the end of this volume.

Preventing Prenatal Harm
Should the State Intervene?

DEBORAH MATHIEU

Department of Political Science, University of Arizona,
Tucson, Arizona, U.S.A.

SPRINGER-SCIENCE+BUSINESS MEDIA, B.V.

Library of Congress Cataloging-in-Publication Data

Mathieu, Deborah.
Preventing prenatal harm : should the state intervene? / by Deborah Mathieu.
p. cm. -- (Clinical medical ethics ; v. 1)
Includes bibliographical references (p.).
ISBN 978-94-017-3745-6 ISBN 978-0-585-27181-1 (eBook)
DOI 10.1007/978-0-585-27181-1
1. Prenatal care--United States--Moral and ethical aspects. 2. Unborn children (Law)--United States. 3. Pregnant women--Legal status, laws, etc.--United States. I. Title. II. Series.
RG960.M33 1991
176--dc20 90-15592

ISBN 978-94-017-3745-6

Printed on acid free paper

Table of Contents

Preface

The issues explored in this book have unfortunately come to be known as 'maternal-fetal conflicts'. The phrase is unsatisfactory because it is misleading: It places the emphasis on the well-being of the fetus instead of on the born child (who will bear the burden of any harm done prenatally); it assumes a conflict between a pregnant women and her offspring (while the issue is usually more complex and more broadly based); and it incorrectly implies that all pregnant women are appropriately regarded as mothers. For these reasons, I have chosen to avoid the phrase 'maternal-fetal conflict' altogether, and will instead speak in terms of 'preventable prenatal harm'. I mention this at the outset, for those of you familiar with 'maternal-fetal conflicts' who might be wondering if I am addressing the same issues. Yes. But I am trying to look at them in a new – and I hope more fruitful – way.

I would like to thank the other participants in the Hastings Center's maternal-fetal project – especially those who disageed with me – for being so thought-provoking. And I owe a lasting debt of gratitude to Henry Ruth and Allen Buchanan for their invaluable counsel.

May 1991 *Deborah Mathieu,*

Notice

Except in the instance of cases that have been reported in the public media or have become public through court hearings, all identifiable information used in case examples has been changed, and the structure of the case examples altered, so as not to identify the individuals involved. Instead, case examples have been constructed out of numerous clinical experiences so as to illustrate a general problem in bioethics, health care delivery, or health care policy. Any similarity to actual individuals living or dead is purely coincidental.

Also, though legal cases and principles are examined in this volume, there is no intention to provide legal advice. For legal advice there is no substitute for directly subvening the legal profession.

Chapter One

Introduction

Picture an infant in the neonatal intensive care unit: He is underdeveloped and tiny for his age, with a malformed spinal cord and a very small head. He suffers from severe diarrhea, he cries constantly – he is extremely irritable – and he never meets your gaze. This is a child born of a crack addict. And picture a low birthweight newborn suffering from heroin withdrawal: She is feverish, hypertonic and respiring rapidly; she trembles constantly and vomits intermittently; her high-pitched cry is incessant, as is her frantic fist-sucking. Now imagine a severely brain-damaged infant whose oxygen supply was cut off during delivery because his mother refused to undergo a cesarean section.

It is natural to feel sympathy for these infants. It is natural also to feel outrage on their behalf: If their mothers had behaved differently, these children could have been born healthy. It is natural to feel, even, that these children were wronged, and that their mothers are culpable. After all, the children's chances for leading independent lives were destroyed through their mothers' actions, and now their futures are in jeopardy.

But how far should we take our sympathy and our outrage? Do we want the state to intervene to seek to prevent these kinds of misfortunes? Do we want the state to use its coercive force to require pregnant women to behave in certain ways? The choice is between respecting a pregnant woman's right to decide what happens to her own body and protecting an innocent child from avoidable damage. In other words, whose interests should the state protect: a woman's interest in remaining free from certain forms of state control or the child's interest in having a decent quality of life?[1]

U.S. law courts have already confronted questions regarding the appropriate treatment of pregnant women who act in ways that are detrimental to the life and/or health of the children they intend to bear, and it is not unusual for the courts to rule against the women. In one of the oldest known cases, the Supreme Court of New Jersey ordered a twenty-three-year old Jehovah's Witness, who was eight months pregnant, to undergo a blood transfusion for the sake of her 'unborn child.' The attending physician had determined that the woman was in danger of severe hemorrhaging, and the court acted because it believed that 'the unborn child is entitled to the law's protection' [289]. The woman left the hospital, however, before the blood transfusion could be administered.

Since then, other pregnant women have been ordered by courts to undergo medical treatments – some of them considerably more invasive than a blood transfusion – for the sake of the children they were planning to bear. Some women have even been ordered to undergo surgery – cesarean sections – believed necessary to save the lives of their term fetuses. In one case, a woman in the thirty-ninth week of pregnancy was diagnosed as having complete placenta previa, a condition which portended, the attending physician claimed, that neither she nor her fetus would survive a vaginal delivery. She refused a cesarean section, however, for religious reasons. The judge who heard the case ruled that the state legislators had intended the juvenile statutes to apply to viable fetuses, and so concluded that this fetus was a 'deprived child' within the meaning of the state juvenile code. The judge then ordered that 'all medical procedures deemed necessary by the attending physician to preserve the life of the defendant's child [be performed]' [274]. Ironically, a cesarean section was ultimately unnecessary, for the woman's condition corrected itself, and the child was delivered alive vaginally.[2]

In Colorado, a thirty-three-year old morbidly obese woman who was near term found herself immersed in a judicial proceeding shortly after admission to the hospital. Her attending physician had recommended a cesarean section because of indications of fetal hypoxia (lack of oxygen), but the woman refused to undergo the operation because of her fear of surgery. In response to a telephone call from the physician, a judge held a hearing at the woman's bedside. The judge ruled that the fetus was a 'dependent and neglected child' within the meaning of the Colorado juvenile code, and ordered the woman to undergo the operation in order to safeguard the life of the term fetus. The woman accepted the judge's decision, and permitted the operation to proceed. On hindsight, the surgery may have been unnecessary: The child to whom she gave birth was much healthier than the physicians had expected (leading them to suspect that their fetal monitoring devices had given them inaccurate information) [30].

Courts have sanctioned other sorts of limitations on pregnant women's liberty as well. A judge in Maryland, for instance, ordered a pregnant woman who was addicted to narcotics to enter a drug treatment program and to submit to weekly urinalysis until the birth of her child. The physician who brought the suit against the woman claimed that her ingestion of a variety of drugs – morphine, cocaine and valium – would 'retard, inhibit, and prevent [the child-to-be's] further growth and development' to a life-threatening degree [237]. In Wisconsin, a judge ordered a near-term teenager to be placed in secure detention until the birth of her child because she lacked 'motivation or ability to seek prenatal care' [181]. And a District of Columbia Superior Court judge ordered a thirty-year old pregnant woman, who was convicted of second-degree theft for passing $721.98 in bad checks, to 180 days in jail in order to protect her fetus from her alleged drug use. Acknowledging the harshness of a six-month sentence for this kind of first offense, the judge explained, 'I'm going to keep her locked up until the baby is born because she tested positive for cocaine when she came before me. She's apparently an addictive personality and I'll be darned if I'm going to have a baby born that way' [42]. The child was born healthy [61].[3]

In a different use of the criminal sanction, criminal charges were brought against a California woman for failing to provide proper care to her son while pregnant with him: She allegedly had taken illegal drugs during pregnancy and had failed to seek medical help in time to prevent the death of her child shortly after birth. The charges in this case were ultimately dropped [113]. But women in Michigan and Ohio have been convicted of child abuse for having ingested heroin while pregnant [267, 270]. And a twenty-three year old woman in Florida, who had given birth to three cocaine-affected infants, was arrested after the birth of a fourth child and convicted of delivering a controlled substance to a minor: Giving her baby cocaine through the umbilical cord. She was sentenced to fifteen years probation, including a year of drug rehabilitation as well as vocational training [61].

These cases raise fundamental ethical, legal, and social policy questions: Should women be coerced into giving up alcohol, cigarettes, and narcotic drugs during pregnancy? Should fetal therapy ever be forced on an unconsenting pregnant woman? Should a mother be punished for having caused serious prenatal harm? Or should she be required to pay damages to the child to compensate for the harm she caused or could have prevented? What role should the courts play? The legislatures? Health care professionals? What are the legal and moral rights at stake here, and the obligations? Which ones are most compelling?

It is fair to say that the new techniques for recognizing and responding to prenatal harms generate a variety of troubling issues which, in turn, pose fundamental challenges to the fields of medicine, biomedical ethics, law, and public policy. And even more questions regarding the appropriate treatment of a pregnant woman and her fetus will arise as new procedures for fetal intervention are developed and perfected. These newly gained options for fetal benefit seriously challenge the traditional view of pregnancy as a personal matter, and challenge as well society's depth of commitment to freedom of choice in general. Indeed, these cases raise in a new and vivid way some of the most basic issues about rights, duties, the moral limits of the law, and the scope of legitimate state action.

Many of these dilemmas exist because we are uncertain how best to utilize our new technologies. It is difficult sometimes to perceive how time-honored methods of dealing with difficult moral choices can come to our aid, when we are faced with new issues for which there are no widely accepted conventions or clearly legitimate expectations. Nor is there any general agreement about our goals – except perhaps for some consensus regarding a few abstract ideals, such as the general value of healthy babies. We need to be more explicit about our purposes here: What are we trying to accomplish? And, of course, we must not forget the most frequently asked question in bioethics: Who should decide whose interests will predominate?

Affecting the Outcome of a Pregnancy

A pregnant woman's actions and omissions, and those of her physician, take on moral significance when the actors have a choice, when there are alternatives available to them. If only one course of action is possible, then their pursuit of that course cannot be construed as morally problematic. Likewise, interventions into pregnant women's activities are rationally justified only when it is possible to affect the outcome of the pregnancy. No one is obligated to make futile efforts to prevent or ameliorate a harm.

Lifestyle Choices

The outcome of a pregnancy can be affected by a variety of interventions, and one approach is to seek to influence a pregnant woman to change her lifestyle in some particular way. Such changes could benefit a great many children, since a wide array of lifestyle choices of pregnant women may have deleterious effects on their offspring. There is some evidence, for instance, that ingesting such seemingly innocuous substances as caffeine and quinine could result in birth defects. And using some common, over-the-counter medications - such as aspirin and cough syrup - may also cause fetal damage [35, 137]. Even the mother's diet can have severely harmful effects on the fetus: Maintaining a diet low in nutrition may cause congenital malformations, brain impairments, and growth retardation [54, 178, 196].

Other lifestyle choices of the pregnant woman can also jeopardize the health of the fetus. Many studies have indicated that consuming alcohol during pregnancy substantially increases the risk of serious harm to the future child: growth-retardation, mental retardation, central nervous system abnormalities, and facial abnormalities [1, 26, 45, 60, 106, 134, 135, 155, 162, 173, 179]. And studies conducted since the 1950s clearly demonstrate the relationship between smoking cigarettes during pregnancy and growth retardation of the child [46, 112, 221]. The growth retardation is generally symmetrical: The newborn weighs less (because of a reduction in lean body mass, not just fat), and is smaller from head to foot. Some physicians consider this symmetrical growth retardation to be a 'fetal tobacco syndrome.' In addition, smoking during pregnancy increases the risk of premature birth and perinatal death, and may cause serious placental complications [64, 139, 213].

The damaging effects of the use of narcotics (codeine, morphine, heroin, and methadone) during pregnancy have been noted for decades. Neonatal drug dependence, for instance, has been well-documented since the turn of the century, and a variety of other risks to the child also have been noted: low birthweight, hyaline membrane disease, and sudden infant death syndrome [6, 65, 87, 90, 102]. Cocaine and crack (a less expensive and more potent form of cocaine) also have negative effects on the children born to addicted mothers: premature birth, low birthweight, emotional and developmental problems, central nervous system disorders, and a variety of malformations (e.g., to the genitals, kidneys, head, intestines, and spinal cord) have been reported [38, 39, 90, 142, 144, 175, 242].

It has been demonstrated, however, that a woman who ceases these activities during pregnancy greatly improves the health of her future child and its chances for survival [12, 49, 64, 135, 176]. This, for some people, is reason enough to conclude that women who engage in these activities should be required to change their lifestyles while they are pregnant. The harm to a woman would be minor, it is contended, compared with the great benefits to her future child. One proposal is to use the threat of criminal prosecution to coerce pregnant women into changing their lifestyle: Legislators could pass laws mandating that women behave in certain ways while pregnant (e.g., refrain from smoking cigarettes and/or drinking alcohol) or face criminal charges [51, 177].

Fetal Therapy

A related area of growing concern involves techniques of fetal therapy. One of the oldest means of fetal therapy is the cesarean section, which is employed to save the life and/or health of the term-fetus in a variety of circumstances: cases of myelomeningocele, respiratory distress, abnormal presentation, maternal herpes infections, AIDS, and placenta previa, among others. And since the early 1960s, physicians have been able to treat a wide assortment of other fetal conditions which would have resulted, had they been left untreated, in serious impairments after birth. The first few successful fetal interventions – blood infusions (to ameliorate hydrops fetalis associated with maternal Rh sensitization) and the administration of steroids (to mitigate respiratory distress syndrome) – have been expanded to include the administration of a wide assortment of other medications and vitamins to the fetus (through the mother). A fetus who cannot properly metabolize biotin (vitamin H), for example, can be given large doses of the vitamin to control this potentially fatal genetic disorder [107]. Even premature birth, one of the major causes of morbidity and mortality in the newborn period, can be prevented in many instances [154].

Medical researchers have also made significant progress in their ability to intervene in the development of potentially devastating genetic defects through surgery, thus preventing the harmful effects of these defects from being fully realized. Among these defects are hydronephrosis (obstruction of the urinary tract), hydrocephalus (excessive cerebrospinal fluid), and congenital diaphragmatic hernia [108, 116]. It is anticipated that advances in the ability to treat anatomic defects of fetuses will continue, and that genetic etiologies of severe disabilities will increasingly come under control: For instance, techniques to correct neural tube defects (such as spina bifida) and limb bud malformations (which impair growth and differentiation of the extremities) are continually being developed. A dramatic extension of this type of therapy is gene surgery, which involves replacing a defective gene with a normally functioning one. Researchers are hopeful that, in the not-too-distant future, a fetus who carries the gene for sickle-cell anemia, for example, could be treated in this manner, and a healthy child would be born in place of a sick one. In addition, the recent genome sequencing project promises even more elegant interventions. By mapping the chemical sequences of human genes, scientists hope to learn more about the fundamental mechanism that governs sub-cellular life, such as how we develop from a single egg, how we age, and why we succumb to certain diseases. The knowledge gained from this research may lead to simpler and more effective treatments for diseases (such as sickle-cell anemia, cystic fibrosis, and hemophilia) than gene replacement, which involves surgery.

The physician who wishes to administer a therapy which would alleviate a severe impairment of the fetus will clash with the pregnant woman who – although she intends to bring the fetus to term – refuses to undergo the treatment. Four factors form the basis of the dilemma in this case: 1) a variety of existing fetal therapies can alleviate seriously deleterious conditions; 2) some pregnant women refuse the administration of these therapies even though the women intend to carry their pregnancies to term; 3) competent adults must give their informed, competent, and voluntary consent before medical treatment can be administered to (or through) them; and 4) women have the legal right to seek abortion. These factors do not imply any particular moral, legal, or policy imperatives, but they raise important questions that must be answered before the legal and policy issues can be fully addressed. Why, for instance, would we even consider coercing a pregnant woman to accept medical treatment against her will when she has the power to make our efforts futile by having an abortion? What are the grounds for thinking that medical treatment should be administered to a fetus despite its mother's objections? Does a fetus have a right to medical care? Does the state (or the mother, or the physician) have an obligation to provide medical care to the fetus? And what are the grounds for thinking that a pregnant woman is free to refuse medical treatment for her fetus? Does she have a legal (or moral) right to be left alone? Would the harm of interfering with her decision outweigh the benefits of interfering?

The use of techniques of fetal therapy is of special significance because it requires us to re-examine old debates that many believe had been settled long ago. It even calls into question an almost sacred tenet of Anglo-American law and contemporary medical ethics: that a competent adult (in this case, the pregnant woman) has an overriding right of self-determination with respect to medical treatment. One of the major thrusts of medical ethics in the past has moved steadily toward reinforcing this right, and defending it against what many saw as a rather pervasive medical paternalism. But new developments in fetal therapy call this legal right into question, and we are now confronted with the apparently inescapable conflict between respect for a pregnant woman's right of self-determination and prevention of serious harm to the child she will bear.

Reproductive Hazards in the Workplace

A third method of affecting the outcome of a pregnancy is by removing women from (or prohibiting fertile women from working in) jobs involving the use of substances believed to cause fetal damage. There are two types of reproductive health hazards in the workplace: Some substances cause damage directly to the developing fetus (teratogenic damage); others cause damage to the parents' reproductive systems, and thus indirectly affect their offspring (mutagenic damage). Several substances commonly found in the workplace – such as lead, ethylene oxide, and vinyl chloride – cause both kinds of damage [44, 123].

Goodyear, Eastman Kodak, Dow, DuPont, American Cyanamid Company, B.F. Goodrich, Johnson Controls, Olin Corporation, General Motors, and other major corporations have responded to evidence concerning reproductive hazards in the workplace by barring women from certain jobs. Although some companies prohibit only pregnant women from working with specific substances, another common exclusionary policy prohibits all females between the ages of sixteen and fifty from working with substances that are believed to be reproductive hazards, unless the women can prove that they are sterile. Proponents of these exclusionary policies argue that they are necessary to protect future generations from serious harm, while critics charge that they unfairly discriminate against women.

The issue of reproductive hazards in the workplace, then, highlights a tension between economic interests (companies want to make profits, women want to have well-paying jobs) and moral interests (women want equal employment opportunities, everyone wants healthy children). Although these interests are not necessarily incompatible, they conflict in those cases in which the risk of reproductive harm is uncertain and/or the cost involved in cleaning up the work environment is prohibitive. In these instances it simply is not feasible to meet all of the interests at stake, and so the policy issue becomes a choice of whose interests will prevail. As with the imposition of fetal therapies, the choice is between two unfortunate outcomes: causing harm to some women in order to seek to prevent harm to their offspring, or permitting harm to befall newborn children in the hope of avoiding harm to their mothers.

Other Methods of Affecting the Outcome of a Pregnancy

Perhaps, though, prenatal harms could best be dealt with after the fact. Rather than intervening in the lives of pregnant women in order to prevent prenatal harms, that is, we might do better to permit the children who had been harmed *in utero* to sue their mothers and/or the responsible health care providers [171, 207, 215]. The child would still be harmed, to be sure, but at least he or she could seek compensation for it. Tort law, then, might be the best method for dealing with these situations. Obviously, this is an important issue here, since any conclusions regarding appropriate actions during pregnancy would be affected profoundly if it is likely that some of the legal and ethical problems posed by prenatal harms could be addressed more successfully after birth.

There are other alternatives as well. One may wish to maintain the status quo: At present, most pregnant women are free to behave however they wish, no matter how injurious their actions are to their future children, and the state offers few inducements to act otherwise. Or, one may wish to develop incentive structures to encourage women (but not to require them) to behave in certain ways during pregnancy.

Status of the Fetus

It might be helpful at this point to consider briefly the moral and legal status of the fetus, and the relevance of this dual status to the issues at hand. Certainly the position one adopts regarding the status of the fetus has a bearing on one's views of the permissibility of abortion (if one regards coherence as a virtue); but the connection between the status of the fetus and grounds for intervening in the life of a pregnant woman to prevent harm to the child she intends to bear is less clear. It is important to put the discussion in its proper context, and to lay the groundwork for further analysis.

Legal Status of the Fetus

Until very recently, the status of the fetus in Anglo-American law was fairly straightforward: A fetus had no legal rights. Indeed, with a few minor exceptions, none of the four areas of law which impact upon the fetus - abortion law, criminal law, tort law, and property law - recognized the fetus as having any legally protectable interests. But state legislators are reconsidering this rule, and on occasion are changing it dramatically. In 1986, Missouri legislators, for instance, amended existing state law to read that 'unborn children have protectable interests in life, health, and well-being,' and to require that all state laws be interpreted to provide fetuses with the same rights enjoyed by other persons [156]. This issue, which is enormously controversial and engenders heated debate, will be on the political agenda for years to come.

Abortion Law

Laws pertaining to abortion have shifted as times and circumstances have changed. Until the mid-nineteenth century, the vast majority of states did not ban abortion before quickening (when the mother can feel the fetus moving, at approximately the sixteenth week of pregnancy); yet by 1900, every state had outlawed abortions except for those necessary to save the life of the mother (although the seriousness of the crime of abortion varied from state to state). The trend began to be reversed again in the late 1960s, and by the time the Supreme Court addressed the abortion issue in 1973, eighteen states had adopted less stringent abortion laws: Four states allowed early abortions to be performed on demand, while fourteen other states permitted abortions to be performed under certain circumstances (danger to the mother's life and physical or mental health, pregnancies due to rape or incest, and serious fetal impairments) [140].

In its landmark 1973 ruling in *Roe v. Wade* [293], the U.S. Supreme Court concluded that a woman has a constitutional right of privacy in her decision whether or not to bear a child, giving her the legal right to terminate her pregnancy (a right even her husband cannot override) [286].

But there are limitations on a woman's reproductive rights: The Court determined that the right to seek an abortion does not include the right to the means to have an abortion, so Congress may legitimately refuse to fund abortions for indigent women [245, 264, 279], and states may legitimately prohibit the use of public facilities and public employees in performing abortions [307].

In addition, the Supreme Court has found a 'compelling state interest' in preserving the 'potentiality of human life,' so a woman's legal right to seek an abortion is sharply curtailed in the final months of pregnancy. Although the Court has consistently rejected the claim that a fetus has any rights under the law, including the right to life, it has determined that at a certain point in its development the fetus ought to be protected:

> All this...persuades us that the word 'person,' as used in the Fourteenth Amendment, does not include the unborn....We need not resolve the difficult question of when life begins. When those trained in the respective disciplines of medicine, philosophy, and theology are unable to arrive at any consensus, the judiciary, at this point in the development of man's knowledge, is not in a position to speculate on the answer....We repeat, however, that the State does have an important and legitimate interest in preserving and protecting the health of the pregnant woman...and that it has still another important and legitimate interest in protecting the potentiality of human life. These interests are separate and distinct. Each grows in substantiality as the woman approaches term and, at a point during pregnancy, each becomes 'compelling' [293].

For sixteen years following the *Roe* decision, the Court consistently held that the state's interest in protecting potential life becomes compelling when the fetus becomes 'viable': that is, when the fetus is 'potentially able to live outside the mother's womb, albeit with artificial aid' [293]. Before fetal viability, abortion is allowed for almost any reason at all; after it, states may choose to permit abortion only when the life or health of the mother is at stake. The Supreme Court has not at any time designated viability as the point at which a fetus becomes a person in the eyes of the law; rather, fetal viability is simply the point at which the state's interest in protecting potential human life becomes compelling, although it is still not compelling enough to outweigh consideration for the life or health of the mother.

But in 1989, the Supreme Court began to allow more state regulation of abortion than had been permissible in the years following the *Roe* ruling, and to shift emphasis away from viability as the critical demarcation point

[307]. Stating that, 'We do not see why the State's interest in protecting human life should come into existence only at the point of viability, and that there should therefore be a rigid line allowing state regulation after viability but prohibiting it before viability,' the Court signalled its willingness to reconsider and perhaps recast the *Roe* model. The Court did not, however, couch any of its arguments or conclusions in terms of fetal rights, nor did it suggest that the fetus had any legal rights.

Criminal Law

In most states, the violent destruction of a fetus of any age without the consent of its mother is not an act of murder. An individual who hits a pregnant woman with a stick, intending to kill her viable fetus and succeeding, could be charged with assault and battery of the woman, but in the majority of states he will not be charged with murder for killing the fetus [220]. The legal response to this type of case does vary from state to state, however, because it depends on judicial interpretation of the particular state's legislation on the matter (as distinguished from judicial interpretation of the common law), and most state statutes do not address the question directly, leaving the courts free to interpret legislative intent. Most courts do so narrowly, claiming that if legislators had wanted to include fetuses within the meaning of the homicide law, they would have done so. Others apply a broader construction – utilizing notions of fairness or considerations of public policy – and in effect redefine the scope of the statutes. In response to the death of an eight and a half month-old fetus in an automobile accident, for example, the Massachusetts Supreme Court ruled in 1984 that a viable fetus is a person within the ambit of that state's motor vehicle homicide law [254]. The court did not find the defendant in that case to be guilty, however, recognizing that its decision 'may have been unforeseeable.'

A few state statutes specifically speak to the issue, making the court's job fairly straightforward. Unhappy with the outcome of a particular case – a man had savagely kneed his estranged and pregnant wife in the stomach, killing the fetus she was carrying; and the court had ruled that he was not guilty of murder because the fetus was not included under the California murder statute [276] – California state legislators responded by designing a compromise of sorts between their belief that a fetus can be murdered and the widely accepted position that the fetus is not a person in the eyes of the law. Hence, rather than defining a fetus as a 'person' (or a 'human being', in the words of the statute), California legislators instead added a new category of murder victim: As amended, the California penal code now avers that 'Murder is the unlawful killing of a human being, or a fetus, with malice aforethought'. And legislators in Minnesota voted in 1986 to impose criminal penalties for the 'murder of an unborn child', which they defined as the 'offspring of a human being conceived, but not yet born'.

Tort Law

All states accept the legal principle that a third party who negligently injures a fetus who is later born alive may be liable for damages [91]. Joel Feinberg explains how a court of law might think through a particular case involving prenatal harm [82, p. 96]:

> A negligent motorist who runs over a pregnant woman may cause damage to the fetus that causes it later to be born deformed or chronically ill. Some time after birth that infant will have an active welfare interest in self-locomotion or health that may be harmed (doomed to defeat) right from the beginning. The child comes into existence in a harmed state caused by the earlier negligence of a motorist whose act initiated the causal sequence, at a point before actual personhood, that later resulted in the harm. The motorist's negligent driving made the actual person, who came into existence months later, worse off than she would otherwise have been. If the motorist had not been negligent, the child would have been undamaged.

As Feinberg's example indicates, courts recognize the harm as befalling the child, not the fetus. In other words, the fetus as such need not be considered to have any legal standing at all in order for the courts to recognize a prenatal harm. Thus prenatal harm suits are not intended to vindicate the rights of the fetus: The courts recognize claims made for compensation on behalf of children who suffered prenatal injuries and were born alive.

The situation is a bit muddier when the tort involves recovery for a negligent prenatal act which results in death (i.e., a 'wrongful death' suit). Some states are quite restrictive: The child must be born alive and then die of injuries wrongfully inflicted to it for a wrongful death action to be recognized. In other states, a wrongful death claim can be made on behalf of an unborn but viable fetus who died because of wrongfully inflicted injuries; while in still others, claims will be recognized for the wrongful death of any fetus regardless of its stage of development [28, 220]. It should be noted, however, that in recognizing wrongful death suits, courts have not thereby conferred an important legal or moral status on the fetus, for the courts consider the harm as having befallen the parents, not the fetus. As the Supreme Court has explained, courts generally allow wrongful death suits in order 'to vindicate the parents' interest and do not confer legal recognition of fetuses as 'persons' in the whole sense' of the term [293, p. 162].

Property Law

Many people mistakenly believe that a fetus may inherit property. But the Uniform Probate Code states that, 'Relatives of the decedent [who are] conceived before his death but [who are] born thereafter inherit as if they had been born in the lifetime of the decedent.' Thus the right to property accrues to the individual who is alive and outside his mother, and the right attaches for inheritance purposes at conception – but only if the fetus survives birth. Hence the fetus itself does not really have a right to property.

Discussion

The fetus is denied significant legal status because it is not considered to be a *person* in the eyes of the law. As the Supreme Court explained in *Roe v. Wade*:

> In areas other than criminal abortion the law has been reluctant to endorse any theory that life, as we recognize it, begins before live birth or to accord legal rights to the unborn except in narrowly defined situations and except when the rights are contingent upon live birth....In short, the unborn have never been recognized in the law as persons in the whole sense [293, pp. 161-162].

This finding has far-reaching implications. One of the most important is that the Fourteenth Amendment to the U.S. Constitution, which applies only to 'persons,' does not apply to the fetus. Hence the fetus does not enjoy equal protection under the law, nor do considerations of due process apply to it.

The U.S. Supreme Court could have decided to declare the fetus to be a person in the eyes of the law. After all, the Court considers corporations to be persons for some purposes: They are persons under the criminal law and the Internal Revenue Code, for instance, and they are protected by the Fourteenth Amendment [258, 281, 298]. But corporations are not persons for all purposes; the right against self-incrimination guaranteed by the Fifth Amendment is not extended to corporations, for example [247].

The Court does not recognize corporations as persons because it sees in corporations some sort of metaphysical being worthy of respect. Instead, this notion of personhood is an artificial construct based on utilitarian considerations: the benefits to society that would accrue by recognizing corporations as persons for some purposes but not for others, and the disbenefits of not doing so. One advantage of recognizing corporations as persons is that significant limitations on government activities are thereby set. If a corporation did not enjoy the fundamental protections of the Fourteenth Amendment, then the state could regulate any business, or even abolish it, for any reason (or for no reason) and with only indirect regard for considerations of fairness as they pertain to the persons who own the artificial entity. But by giving a corporation separate legal status, the Court ensures that the state abides by those minimum standards that society considers to be of fundamental importance, such as the provisions of the Fourteenth Amendment. This also serves to protect the individuals - owners, shareholders and employees - who comprise the corporation and who are, in their own right, persons under the law.

In deciding whether to accord fetuses the status of persons, the Supreme Court also took social costs into account. Were the fetus considered to be a person, according to the Supreme Court's opinion in *Roe v. Wade*, its 'right to life would then be guaranteed specifically by the [Fourteenth] Amendment' [293, pp. 156-157]. This would mean that most abortions would be tantamount to murder, and, to be logically consistent and maintain any legal integrity, it would also mean that the mothers, physicians, and nurses involved in abortion would have to be prosecuted for murder.[4] Besides creating a new class of criminal, outlawing abortion would have other severely deleterious effects on women. In deciding *Roe*, the Court noted the possible mental, physical, and financial harms to women because of unwanted pregnancies:

> The detriment that the state would impose upon the pregnant woman by denying choice altogether is apparent. Specific and direct harm medically diagnosable even in early pregnancy may be involved. Maternity, or additional offspring, may force upon the woman a distressful life and future. Psychological harm may be imminent. Mental and physical health may be taxed by child care. There is also the distress, for all concerned, associated with the unwanted child, and there is the problem of bringing a child into a family already unable, psychologically and otherwise, to care for it. In other cases, as in this one, the additional difficulties and continuing stigma of unwed motherhood may be involved [293, p. 153].

In *Roe v. Wade*, therefore, the Court seems to have been persuaded that the advantages to society of maintaining the status quo – in which fetuses are not persons in the eyes of the law – outweigh the disadvantages.

The current legal view of the fetus, which denies the fetus any significant rights, is also based on the belief that the fetus is not the sort of being to whom rights naturally accrue. But this position is being challenged, and some people claim that the fetus should be recognized as having many of the same rights as other human beings. It is time, they argue, to alter the law to reflect the normative view of the fetus as a member of the moral community and a bearer of rights (although what these rights are, and when in its development the fetus comes to possess them, remain matters of disagreement).

The Moral Status of the Fetus

A human fetus is a human being insofar as it is a member of the species *homo sapiens*, with the genetic structure typical of our species. And since it is alive, it is a living human being. For many, this statement is factually true but morally irrelevant. For others it is an important moral claim indeed, because for them, the question 'When does human life begin?' is identical to the question 'When does moral personhood begin?' Since a fetus is a living human being, some people conclude that it is also a being with a moral and legal right to life.

It is crucial to note, however, that the question of whether a fetus is a member of our species is not the same as the question of whether it is a full-fledged member of our moral community (a 'person'). The former is a matter of fact, the latter is a normative judgment. Because the concept of a 'person' is a moral status concept, the issue of whether the fetus is a person is not a scientific or medical question to be settled simply by appeal to ontogeny or embryology. Indeed, two people can agree on the scientific facts about fetal development and still disagree fiercely on the moral status of the fetus. Identifying the human fetus as a person in the moral sense, then, is a normative assertion, not a statement of fact. Moreover, the fact that the fetus is a member of the species *homo sapiens* does not entail the conclusion that it is a member of the moral community of persons, for the opposite conclusion is equally plausible. Hence the fundamental question remains: Is the fetus a person in the moral sense?[5]

To say that a being is a person is to recognize him or her as fully a member of the moral community. More specifically, a person in the moral sense is a being who has basic moral rights, including the right to life. These moral rights are the basis for most legal rights. If we reflect on the paradigm cases in ordinary life in which we most confidently ascribe personhood to a being, we notice that we associate a certain descriptive content (e.g., self-awareness, ability to choose and to act on reasons, capacity to feel pleasure and pain) with the moral concept of a person.[6] These qualities are given moral weight because they are related to life within the moral community, to the reasons behind the strictures of morality and the requirements of law.

But the concept of a person in the moral sense remains ill-defined and controversial insofar as we cannot agree on its boundaries. While most would agree that the concept refers to beings who are worthy of respect and who enjoy certain fundamental moral rights, there is not much consensus beyond these vague designations. Considerable disagreement, for example, still exists as to whether the term 'person' refers only to those beings who can be morally responsible for their actions (the paradigm case), or if it also includes beings who have the potential for being morally responsible for their actions, or if it includes as well all beings (regardless of their capacities and potentialities) who are members of the same species as those who can be morally responsible for their actions, or if it includes all beings who meet only some of the qualifications (such as the ability to experience pleasure and pain).

It has been suggested that the utilization of recently developed techniques of fetal therapy would confer the status of personhood on the fetus. As one commentator asks, 'If the fetus can be treated, then is it a patient? If it is a patient, then is it a person?' [110]. And another responds, 'Treatment of the fetus...seems to confer on the fetus the status of patient, someone with rights, interests, and claims upon us which should be protected' [199]. In other words, some people are suggesting that our ability to treat the fetus therapeutically may help define its moral status and our obligations toward it.

This, however, is simply not the case: The ability to treat a fetus as a patient has no bearing whatsoever on its status as a person, nor does it reflect any light on what our obligations to the fetus should be. Not all patients are persons: A doctor may administer antibiotics to a cat, or operate on a mouse, but the ability to perform these procedures does not itself confer any moral status at all on the beings undergoing them. In addition, procedures to relieve fetal distress have existed for centuries, and the development of new and different therapies does not make the fetus any more of a person than it has been. The question of what we owe the fetus is not a technological one, but a moral one.

There are four basic ways of viewing the moral status of the human fetus: 1) the fetus is a person throughout its development; 2) the fetus gains the moral status of a person at some point in its development: e.g., the appearance of brain waves, the ability to feel pain, viability, and so on; 3) the fetus does not have the moral status of a person, and indeed has no moral status at all; or 4) the fetus does have some moral standing, although it is not a full-fledged person.[7] All of the suggestions for the onset of personhood are somewhat arbitrary, and necessarily so. One reason for this is that the transition from a fertilized egg to a mentally competent adult (the paradigm case of a moral person) is a continuous development, not a series of discrete stages with abrupt transitions. The question, 'When does personhood begin?' is similar to the question, 'When does adulthood begin?' We decide that someone is adult enough to drive a car at the age of sixteen, adult enough to vote at eighteen, adult enough to drink liquor at twenty-one. But when is that individual really an adult? We draw lines for social and/or legal purposes; but we must recognize that they are, in part, conventional stipulations – decisions of social policy. This is true also of any decision we may make regarding when in its development, if ever, a fetus becomes a person in the moral sense. But simply because the point at which we confer personhood on a being is in part arbitrary, it does not follow that it is inappropriate or wrong to do so. It simply means that, although the judgment is grounded in sound reasons, it is also partially subjective and thus it cannot satisfy everyone. Once we recognize this, perhaps, the question of the moral status of the fetus will cease being an occasion for sterile polemic and will open itself to reasoned resolution.

However, no public consensus seems forthcoming, or even likely, concerning the controversy over the moral status of the fetus. This contentious debate will not be furthered here, either, for I shall not argue for or against the moral status of the fetus. It simply is not necessary to posit that the human fetus is a person in order to be able to argue that it should be treated in certain ways if it is being carried to term. Indeed, although the moral status of the fetus plays a significant role in the controversy over abortion, it is largely irrelevant to the issue of the prevention of prenatal harms.

Analyzing the Problem

Most commentators have analyzed the problem of preventable prenatal harms in terms of a conflict between a pregnant woman and her fetus. One conclusion is that a physician sometimes has 'an obligation to the fetus that could not be waived by the mother' [141]; while an equally plausible alternative is that 'It is wrong to allow obstetrics or the state to subsume the interests and the civil rights of pregnant women to those of the products of conception within them' [198]. These views of the dilemma are clearly colored by different views of the moral status of the fetus: In one instance, the fetus is given significant moral status, in the other it has the value of a mere body part. But any attempt to present the debate over preventable prenatal harms in this manner – that is, to view it in terms of a maternal-fetal conflict – is doomed to failure. The problem is that the issue on which the debate thereby rests – the moral status of the fetus – is a matter of great controversy, and one that is far from being resolved.

Assuming Something About the Moral Status of the Fetus

One problem with analyzing the debate over preventable prenatal harms in terms of a maternal-fetal conflict, then, is that it will inevitably bog down in preliminary arguments over the moral status of the fetus, making any resolution of the problem at hand highly unlikely. Yet it is not just the controversial nature of the moral status of the fetus that stands in the way of a resolution of the dilemma at hand: A social consensus on the moral status of the fetus would do little to help.

Assume, for a moment, that a general agreement has emerged that a fetus is a 'person' in the moral sense. Since a fetus is now considered to possess many of the same moral and legal rights as other persons, it seems to follow that the state should act to protect its rights (especially the fundamental and universal right not to be harmed). But this argument simply will not stand up to scrutiny. For even if the fetus were a person, and possessed a right not to be harmed, it would not necessarily follow that the state should act to protect that right, since the state must balance this right against the rights and interests of the pregnant woman, including her right to decide what happens to her own body. At most, conferring moral and/or legal personhood on the fetus would ground a *prima facie* case for arguing that the state should act in its behalf – but this conclusion needs to be buttressed by other arguments (arguments which are strong enough to outweigh the power of the various countervailing considerations based on the pregnant woman's rights).

Let us assume, now, that there is general agreement that the fetus is not a person, indeed, that its moral status is quite low. Would it follow that a pregnant woman has *carte blanche* to act any way she wishes while she is pregnant? No. One may consistently hold that a fetus has no moral or legal rights, and still argue that a pregnant woman should not be allowed to cause severe and avoidable prenatal harm.

The basis of this position is the belief that the effects of her actions on the health of her *future child*, not on the health of her fetus, are what matter (at least to those for whom the fetus is of little moral concern). If a woman continues her pregnancy to term, then a child will be born who will bear the consequences of whatever happened to it *in utero*. In those cases in which a child is born, another person is involved: a person who has the same moral and many of the same legal rights that his mother has, including the right not to be harmed. Thus even if a fetus is not considered to be a person in the moral or legal sense, there still are important interests of a person which must be weighed against those of the pregnant woman: the interests of her future child. It is for the sake of the child that the fetus will become that a pregnant woman should act. Her obligations, in other words, are to her future child, not to her fetus.

Moral Obligations

The argument that a woman is not free to behave in any way she wishes while she is pregnant is based on the conviction that she is (sometimes) morally responsible for the condition of the child to whom she gives birth.[8] This position is simply an extrapolation from the widely accepted general moral obligations to refrain from harming others (the duty of nonmaleficence) and to contribute to the welfare of others (the duty of beneficence).

There is a chance that every pregnancy will go to term. For this reason, a pregnant woman incurs some moral responsibility for the condition of the future child from the beginning of the pregnancy. This does not mean that she is morally obligated to act always in the best interests of her future child, for her responsibilities are necessarily limited: They must be weighed against her other responsibilities (to herself and perhaps to her other children, her spouse, her employer). Concern for these other responsibilities may even lead a woman to decide to terminate her pregnancy. But if the pregnant woman is free to have an abortion and does not do so, then she has chosen not to avoid a situation in which she will affect the well-being of another person (the child she will bear), and in so choosing she can be deemed to have assumed moral responsibility for at least some aspects of the well-being of that future person.[9]

It is important to note that the pregnant woman's duties are to the post-fetal person the fetus will become *if* it is carried to term: She has no obligations to the fetus *qua* fetus. Consequently, even though a pregnant woman has a moral duty to refrain from causing harm to her future child, she has no duty to bring that child into being. In other words, there is no suggestion here that the fetus has any rights, including the right to receive medical treatment or the right to be born [81].

It is important to note that I am not arguing that a pregnant woman should or should not be compelled to act in certain ways, nor am I suggesting that a public policy setting out limitations on a pregnant woman's freedom of choice would be appropriate. Such conclusions would be premature: There is a notable divergence between acts which are morally required and acts which should be legally required. Indeed, acts which may be regarded as ethically proper in particular instances may at the same time be considered as inappropriate when expanded to the level of social policy. Actions which may prevent harm on an individual level may produce even greater harm if that type of action became a general practice, for instance, or some other arrangement might be more effective in reducing the harm. In other words, it makes perfect sense to hold on the one hand that an action is morally right, and hold on the other hand that it should not be instituted as social (legal) policy. Thus further reasons are needed to justify state involvement in these cases.

So far I have simply noted some general (and fairly vague) conclusions about a woman's moral duties: I believe she is morally obligated to act in the interests of her future child throughout her pregnancy. But I am very far from saying anything at all about her legal duties. The most reasonable conclusion might be that she has no legal duties with regard to her future child – and thus the state may not interfere with her liberty in order to prevent her from causing serious prenatal harm. This complex subject will be addressed at length in Chapters Two, Three, and Four. First, though, it is important to address a common objection to even considering state intervention in these cases: that the Supreme Court's ruling in *Roe v.*

Wade, which gives a woman the legal right to seek an abortion, makes otiose any discussion of state intervention to prevent prenatal harm.

A Woman's Legal Right to Seek an Abortion

According to some commentators, it is unreasonable to posit that the state could legitimately prevent prenatal harms by overriding a pregnant woman's freedom of choice, since the state's recognition of a pregnant woman's legal right to have an abortion is inconsistent with a policy of encouraging or requiring her to act in certain ways.[10] As long as a woman may legally abort her fetus, it is contended, she cannot be compelled to undergo medical treatment or lifestyle changes on its behalf.

If a woman is allowed to seek an abortion, it does seem to make sense to allow her also to act in any way she wishes with regard to her fetus. After all, since a pregnant woman is permitted to sever her relationship with the fetus entirely, how can she legally be enjoined to curtail her activities to avoid harming it? Since abortion is allowed, would it not make more sense (and be more consistent), also to allow other sorts of harm to the fetus?

If we ask the questions in this manner, then of course the answer is that the state may not interfere. But these are not the right questions. Recall that our concern is *not* with the condition of the fetus, but with the condition of the *born child* – a person whose interests the state should protect.

It would be a mistake to assume that a woman's legal right to seek an abortion determines all of her reproductive rights and responsibilities: A woman's right to have an abortion does *not* imply the right to refuse to provide medical treatment to a child she intends to bear; and an obligation to refrain from causing prenatal harm does *not* imply an obligation to forgo having an abortion. Instead, a pregnant woman's obligation to change her lifestyle or to undergo medical treatment for the sake of the child she intends to bear is logically independent of her right to have an abortion. Thus it is reasonable to conclude that, although a woman has the right to abort her fetus, she does not have the liberty to cause serious harm to the child she intends to bear.

A significant advantage of this position is that it is consistent with current Anglo-American law in two important respects: 1) The law does not recognize the fetus as a person; and 2) it does recognize the wrongfulness of prenatal negligent acts or omissions which show up later as injuries to a child. This is not something that is appropriately included within that notorious class of 'legal fictions,' but instead is a logical and principled position based on the consideration that, although the harm was caused while the person was *in utero*, the person now born is the one who suffers it.

The Plan

The conclusion so far is that 1) a pregnant woman has some moral obligations to act in the interests of her future child; 2) it is not inconsistent to allow abortion yet disallow certain activities during pregnancy that would harm future children; 3) the moral status of the fetus is largely irrelevant to the prevention of prenatal harms, and therefore 4) we need not assume anything about the moral status of the human fetus, or argue the moral and legal merits of a woman's right to seek an abortion, in order to determine her other reproductive responsibilities (if any). For our purposes, therefore, the controversy over the fetus's moral status will remain unaddressed. Indeed, harm to the fetus *per se* is not at issue here; our concern, instead, is with those prenatal negligent acts or omissions which show up later as injuries to the child. Surely we can all agree that the born child is a being of significant moral worth who deserves our concern and perhaps even our protection. The question for us is: Ought the state intervene in the lives of pregnant women in order to prevent serious prenatal harms?

There are four stages during which the state can act to prevent prenatal harms: 1) before the woman becomes pregnant (e.g., by forbidding fertile women to work in certain jobs known to cause reproductive damage); 2) during pregnancy (e.g., by requiring that pregnant women refrain from engaging in certain activities known to be hazardous to the fetus, such as imbibing alcohol); 3) during delivery (e.g., by requiring her to undergo a cesarean section); and 4) after the child is born (e.g., by allowing the injured child to sue his mother and/or others for damages, or by prosecuting the mother for having caused harm to her child). Should the state use its power to impose on any woman any of these (or other) methods of affecting the outcome of her pregnancy?

Three very different responses to these questions will be examined: 1) A pregnant woman has both moral and legal obligations to act in the interests of her child-to-be, obligations which the state should uphold; 2) The state should uphold *some* of a woman's moral obligations to her future child;

and 3) While a pregnant woman may have moral obligations to act in the interests of the child she intends to bear, these obligations should *not* be backed by the coercive power of the state. Each of these stances raises profound and perplexing ethical, legal and public policy issues, and all will be explored here.

Some commentators have suggested that the issues at stake can readily be resolved by a straightforward appeal to individual rights. One view is that the state's recognition of a woman's right to decide what happens to her own body is inconsistent with a policy of encouraging or requiring fetal therapy. A very different position is that a child has a right to be born healthy and that the state should be empowered to act to protect this right, even if it means overriding a woman's right of self-determination. Obviously, the espousal of one of these rights rather than the other leads to a very different conclusion regarding the proper role of the state and the culpability of the pregnant woman.

Such a simple rights-based approach, however, provides no adequate resolution of these problems. Instead, the rights-principles must be refined, weighed against one another, and applied within a complex framework of moral values, legal considerations, practical issues, and attention to consequences. In what follows, then, I will offer a pluralistic approach to the problems which does not rest upon a single moral value and does not attempt to solve subtle moral issues by exclusively focusing on rights-principles, much less on one right, but which instead reflects an intricate mixture of moral, legal, and practical concerns. My hope is not to offer the perfect solution to the dilemmas at hand: Such a solution does not exist.[11] Nor do I attempt to offer a grand theory about the proper relationship between the individual and the state in all matters: That ambition is beyond the scope of this essay. My goal, instead, is to analyze the problem of preventable prenatal harms and to offer good reasons – rather than political slogans or emotional reactions – for determining which alternatives are superior to others.

Law and Morality

Although many of the issues at stake raise important legal questions, they do not involve exclusively legal matters, and it is important to resist the tendency to transform discussions of moral problems into arguments about legal liability. Although the latter is important, it cannot resolve the ethical questions that arise.

Practical considerations alone dictate that we should not look exclusively to the law for guidance. Sometimes the law has nothing to say on the matter: Rapid technological advances in medicine, for instance, may create new ethical dilemmas which the law simply has not yet addressed. And even those issues with which the law has grappled may be open to considerable dispute, since the conclusions are sometimes ambiguous, if not actually contradictory.

There is another, more basic reason for distinguishing ethics from law. All forms of law – common law constructed by judges, statutory law, judicial interpretations of statutory law, administrative regulations, executive orders – are subject to ethical criticism. Although the law is not the servant of morality – i.e., there are many instances in which we do not want to hold someone legally responsible for his actions though we find him morally blameworthy – there are moral constraints on how we can apply the law [70, 82]. Hence one of my primary goals is to develop a moral foundation on which a legal framework can rest.

Yet the state of the law is important, of course, and reference will be made to it whenever appropriate. With regard to the issues at hand, the common law tends to be the most germane, and the greatest scope of illustrative legal cases comes from the American system. There are a variety of reasons for this: Americans seem to be quite litigious, and they often look to the courts to make their difficult decisions for them, while American lawyers (including prosecutors) seek not only justice but personal reputation through the courts and so are willing to pursue unusual cases. Whatever the impetus for pursuing court action, the fact remains that American common law offers a bountiful source of cases and precedents. Since my objective is not legal analysis but rather a probing of the foundations of law and public policy, the legal cases will be used primarily as heuristic devices.

Outline of the Book

The object of this chapter has been to provide the background information and analyses of basic issues that are essential for understanding the arguments explored in the following chapters. I have not argued that the status quo – where most pregnant women are free to act in any way they wish, regardless of the harm they cause to the children they bear – should be changed in any particular direction, or even that it should be changed at all. My point has been, rather, that these are open questions; and my objective in this chapter has been to explore some of the basic concepts, values, and issues at stake in this complex discussion.

Using the conclusions drawn here, Chapters Two and Three will explore arguments for and against coercing pregnant women to behave in certain ways: Chapter Two analyzes the reasons in favor of limiting individual liberty in order to prevent prenatal harm, whereas Chapter Three discusses reasons against such policies. These chapters are fairly abstract, focusing on general moral and legal principles and on public policy issues, and hence they are inconclusive: Although various arguments are explored, no final adjudication is made as to which position is strongest. This is the goal of Chapter Four, which is much more concrete: It applies the arguments presented in the earlier chapters to specific cases, and argues for particular conclusions. Chapter Four also explores an alternative response to preventable prenatal harms which involves very limited state interference with individual decision making.

Notes

[1] I am speaking here – as I will throughout the book – of born children, not of fetuses. The reasons for this will be presented later in the chapter.

[2] The outcome in this case prompted many people to question the accuracy of the original diagnosis.

[3] Not all cocaine-abusing pregnant women give birth to cocaine-impaired children [68].

[4] And what would happen to the hapless assistant in an *in vitro* fertilization clinic who drops a petri dish of human zygotes? Would she be prosecuted for manslaughter?

[5] Analysis of this controversial question is necessarily brief; for further discussion see [20, 83, 84, 210].

[6] Joel Feinberg suggests that, 'In the commonsense way of thinking, persons are those beings who, among other things, are conscious, have a concept and awareness of themselves, are capable of experiencing emotions, can reason and acquire understanding, can plan ahead, can act on their plans, and can feel pleasure and pain' [84, p. 262].

And Mary Anne Warren [232] proposes the following criteria for personhood:

> 1. consciousness (of objects and events external and/or internal to the being), and in particular the capacity to feel pain; 2. reasoning (the developed capacity to solve new and relatively complex problems); 3. self-motivated activity (activity which is relatively independent of either genetic or direct external control); 4. the capacity to communicate by whatever means, messages of an indefinite variety of types, that is, not just with an indefinite number of possible contents, but on indefinitely many topics; 5. the presence of self-concepts, and self-awareness, either individual or social, or both.

Although these suggestions for the descriptive content of the concept of personhood differ in detail, they are unanimous in relying on cognitive ability – as opposed to membership in a species – as the morally relevant criterion.

[7] It is important to note at this juncture that, while persons are the only beings who enjoy a full complement of rights, they are not the only beings who count morally. Some beings who are not usually considered to be persons – such as cows and pigs – may have moral status, though of a different kind. Simply because they are capable of pleasure and pain they deserve moral consideration, even though they may lack many of the rights that persons have.

[8] A woman who gives birth to a child she never intended to bear is not free from moral responsibility for the condition of that child. However, a woman is not always morally responsible for the condition of the child to whom she gives birth: There may be extenuating circumstances which could relieve her of responsibility.

[9] So H.T. Engelhardt, Jr., suggests that, 'The very availability of abortion, perhaps paradoxically for some, has increased the plausibility of maternal duties to fetuses in that a woman's continuing with a pregnancy is more of an expression of free choice than was the case in the past' [75]. This will be discussed further in Chapter Three.

[10] John Fletcher, for example, worries about the 'inconsistency of encouraging fetal therapy on the one hand and respecting parental choice on the other' [92], while Marc Lappé suggests that, 'Whatever social, medical, or legal sanctions existed for protecting the fetus against potential abuse during pregnancy in the past now may have been seriously compromised by the Supreme Court's abortion decision' [130]. And Robert Blank cautions that, 'In the not-so-remote future, the Court must resolve the logical inconsistency of holding a woman responsible for harming her fetus but not for terminating its existence' [25].

[11] The degree of difficulty presented by the issues I address is nicely illustrated by the workings of one hospital ethics committee [143]. In the spring of 1985, the committee was asked to develop a hospital policy for dealing with pregnant women who refuse blood transfusions, thereby jeopardizing their own lives as well as the lives of their fetuses. The initial reaction of the committee was a compromise of sorts: Before the third trimester, the woman's decision should be determinative; once the pregnancy has entered the final trimester, however, the case should be taken to court or, if it is an emergency, the transfusion should be administered.

The committee was still exploring the subject a year later, and it decided to invite outside experts to participate in the deliberations. The first speaker was a lawyer who argued against coercing pregnant women to accept medical treatment, and her remarks persuaded the committee to alter the proposed policy. The committee provisionally agreed to delete all specific references to pregnant women, choosing instead to include them implicitly in other categories (e.g., competent adults, emancipated minors, and so on). A month later, two obstetricians spoke and they argued for the opposite conclusion: They would seek a court order to transfuse these pregnant women.

For the next few months, the committee wavered over the policy, at times deciding to amend it once again by reinserting a separate section dealing with pregnant women and, at times, deciding to omit any such section. When the committee finally decided that a separate section was indeed appropriate, it could not agree on the particular provisions. By the following spring, after two years of discussion, the committee still had not formulated a final policy on this issue. As one committee member describes the situation:

> It became clear that specific guidelines for pregnant Jehovah's Witnesses could not be formulated. Committee members identified two apparent reasons for the impossibility. First, when it comes to weighing the relative 'interests' or 'rights' of the woman and the fetus, the stage of pregnancy inevitably influences the balance. The solution of opting for either extreme – respect for the rights of the woman or the fetus – was unacceptable to everyone. Second, and more importantly, the problem of ascribing rights and determining their precedence has not been resolved by the larger society. It is unreasonable, therefore, to expect a procedurally oriented policy to resolve a dilemma for which no substantive ethical solution has been forthcoming.
>
> Reluctantly, the committee adopted the suggestion that it not even attempt to dictate a policy but limit its task to describing the competing principles, leaving the decision-making process to the patient and clinician [143, p. 20].

The final version of the policy was adopted in June, 1987. It read:

> Competent adult patients have the right to refuse medical treatment. This right extends to pregnant women. However, some members of society assert that the fetus has 'interests' or 'rights' that compete with the rights of the mother to control her own body. In general, the rights of the mother are clearly acknowledged to take precedence in early pregnancy. As gestation advances, it becomes increasingly difficult for some members of society to ignore the 'interests of the fetus.' Because of the dilemma that arises out of these opposing interests, physicians have an obligation to disclose from the outset if, under specified circumstances, they would be unable to honor a patient's wishes [143, p. 20].

In other words, the committee decided not to formulate a policy, but instead to leave the decisions to the individuals involved. This result is not surprising, for these cases raise some of the most profound and perplexing dilemmas in bioethics and health policy.

Chapter Two

Arguments in Favor of Coercing a Pregnant Woman to Act in the Interests of her Future Child

When a pregnant woman acts or fails to act (including refusing medical care) in a way that will harm the child she intends to bear, her physician has five courses of action available: accept her decision and treat her accordingly; transfer her to another physician who will accede to her wishes; try to persuade her to accept his recommendation; negotiate a compromise plan of action; or ask a court to order her to comply with the recommended treatment. Overriding a mentally competent woman's right to refuse treatment without prior court approval is not a viable alternative: Not only would this course of action violate her rights, but it would expose the physician to civil and criminal liability.[1]

A physician has at present no legal obligation to pursue court involvement in what ordinarily is a private treatment decision, but many physicians feel morally obligated to do so. In a 1987 survey of the heads of fellowship programs in maternal-fetal medicine and of the directors of divisions of maternal-fetal medicine, for instance, forty-six percent of the respondents said that a woman who refused medical advice and thereby endangered the life of her fetus should be detained in a hospital in order to ensure compliance; forty-seven percent supported court orders for invasive procedures – such as cesarean sections and interuterine transfusions – which could be expected to save the life of a fetus who will be carried to term [125].

Which cohort of physicians is right? Should the courts coerce pregnant women into undergoing medical treatment? Or are the women free to make their own choices?

Chapter One argued that a pregnant woman is morally obligated to act in the interests of the child she will bear (whether her moral obligations involve undergoing invasive medical procedures will be discussed later). Now, however, our concern is with the grounds for believing that at least some of a pregnant woman's moral obligations should also be regarded as legal obligations. In other words, are there good reasons for holding that the state may interfere in the life of a pregnant woman in order to prevent prenatal harm? If there are not – if we conclude that state involvement should not even be considered – then a characterization of a woman's moral obligations to act in the interests of the child she intends to bear, while valuable, will have no policy implications.

State Intervention

There are two sources of state power to interfere with a pregnant woman's autonomy in order to prevent prenatal harms: police power and *parens patriae* power.

> The police power is the state's inherent plenary power both to prevent its citizens from harming one another and to promote all aspects of public welfare....The *parens patriae* power, by contrast, is the state's limited paternalistic power to protect or promote the welfare of certain individuals, like young children and mental incompetents, who lack the capacity to act in their own best interests [66, p. 1156].

That the state *can* interfere to prevent harm or promote well-being in certain instances is obvious. The important question is: Under what circumstances is it legitimate for the state to do so? Is it legitimate, for instance, for the state to interfere with a pregnant woman's activities in order to prevent harm to or promote the well-being of her future child? Is it legitimate to make criminal certain activities of pregnant women because they cause prenatal harms?

The fact that the state has the power to limit the choices of pregnant women plus the contention that pregnant women have moral obligations to take reasonable care of the fetuses they intend to carry to term are not enough to justify coercive state intervention to prevent prenatal harms. The belief that a particular action is morally proper is not a conclusive basis for constructing social policy, and additional reasons are needed to justify state involvement in these cases.

Three types of supporting arguments are available. The first is a consequentialist argument: Preventing certain types of prenatal damage creates more good than harm overall. The second type of argument involves the rights of the future child: One could argue, for instance, that a child has a right to begin life with a sound mind and body, or one could base an argument on the more general right not to be harmed, a right that is enforceable as to conduct occurring before birth. For those who remain unconvinced by assertions of rights, a third type of argument is available. This position is based on the premise that a pregnant woman is obligated to meet certain standards of care for the sake of her future child, even if the child has no corresponding rights to such care, and that these obligations should be enforced by the state. We shall deal, in turn, with each of these types of arguments.

An Appeal to Consequences

The basic consequentialist argument is simply that if we permit pregnant women to do as they please – to ingest alcohol or cocaine, to refuse prenatal care, to work with chemicals known to cause teratogenic damage – then we at the same time permit grave harm to befall tens of thousands of innocent beings each year: the children to whom the women give birth. Much of this harm could be prevented and, because it causes so much suffering, many people conclude that it *should* be prevented.

Consider, for example, the case of a pregnant woman who pays insufficient attention to controlling her diabetes. Not only is her own health at risk, but she greatly increases the chances that her child will be born prematurely and with severe malformations. Since both the woman and her child reap the benefits of her adherence to a strict treatment regimen, and since the serious harms to both can easily be avoided, it makes sense, according to a utilitarian calculation, to require the woman in this instance to take her medications and keep to her diet.

This type of utilitarian reckoning, which is concerned with the benefits to individuals in particular, is buttressed by considerations of the benefits to society in general. The high costs of treatment in neonatal intensive care units (which average approximately $2000 a day) would be reduced, mitigating the financial burden on private insurance companies, the hospitals that often must absorb much of the cost, and the taxpayers who fund Medicaid programs (which cover the hospital costs for many indigent children).[2] In addition, the expense and difficulties of institutionalizing mentally and physically handicapped individuals would also decrease – as would the demands for special education programs – as the numbers of severely handicapped individuals dwindle. At the same time the numbers of productive, self-supporting, tax-paying citizens would increase.[3] Thus, it could be argued, society would benefit more were the state to intervene in the activities of pregnant women than were it to allow pregnant women the freedom of choice they have enjoyed in the past.

On these grounds, then, one could argue both that a pregnant women has a moral obligation to refrain from causing prenatal harm (because the benefits to the child outweigh the disbenefits to her), and that the state may enforce this obligation (because the benefits to society at large outweigh the disbenefits to pregnant women). So there are good utilitarian arguments for permitting state intervention in order to prevent at least some cases of serious prenatal harm.

But how much weight should we give these arguments? The answer, of course, is a matter of great controversy. One set of countervailing considerations involves the rights of the pregnant women: Many people in our society believe that an individual's fundamental rights may not be abridged for utilitarian purposes, since these rights outweigh considerations of social benefit. State intervention into the lives of pregnant women, according to this line of thought, would be permitted only insofar as it does not interfere with the women's constitutional rights. But it should be noted that the debate does not end here, for we first must determine which rights a pregnant woman enjoys, and whether these rights indeed outweigh the social benefits of preventing prenatal harms. In addition, the rights of the pregnant women are not the only rights at stake. If children have rights that accrue during the fetal stage, and if pregnant women have corresponding obligations to honor those rights, then the consequentialist arguments in favor of limiting the mother's choices will be strengthened considerably.

The designation of the scope and limits of these rights thus plays an important role in our discussion, and it is fair to say that the consequentialist arguments can be assessed accurately only in light of them. In the following chapter, we shall explore the rights of the pregnant woman; this chapter examines the alleged rights of future persons.[4]

Arguments Based on the Rights of Future Persons

Our increased awareness of the causes of prenatal harms and the development of new techniques for preventing the maturation of serious defects while the child is *in utero* have led some people to assert two rights of the future person: the right to begin life with a sound mind and body, and the right not to be harmed. Either (or both) of these rights might be invoked to justify state intervention into the lives of pregnant women without their consent.[5]

In *Smith v. Brennan* [297], a 1960 case involving a child who was born with deformed feet and legs caused by the effects of an automobile accident which occurred while he was still *in utero*, the New Jersey Supreme Court ruled that,

> Justice requires that the principle be recognized that a child has a legal right to begin life with a sound mind and body. If the wrongful conduct of another interferes with that right, and it can be established by competent proof that there is a causal connection between the wrongful interference and the harm suffered by the child when born, damages for such harm should be recoverable by the child.

In this ruling, the court appeared to go beyond the usual finding of prenatal harm to posit a 'legal right to begin life with a sound mind and body.' Similarly, the New York Supreme Court in *Park v. Chessin* [283] held that there is a 'fundamental right of a child to be born as a whole, functional human being.'[6]

One important question, of course, is whether or not a person does indeed have an inalienable and primary right to begin life with a sound mind and body. Although the *Smith* court announced the right, the actual holding states that damages were recoverable because the automobile accident caused harm to the child while he was still *in utero*. In other words, the court recognized a fairly straightforward tort and probably did not mean to create a new category of right separate and apart from traditional tortious acts that cause identifiable harm.

It has been proposed, however, that the right to begin life with a sound mind and body should be interpreted more broadly and more dramatically. One commentator, for instance, suggests that the court's ruling 'would seem to establish the principle that the child's right to a healthy life takes precedence over the parents' right to reproduce' [207, p. 95]. Understood in this manner, the right to begin life with a sound mind and body would potentially be a powerful means of championing the welfare of children and limiting the freedom of parents (especially pregnant women).

How should the parameters of such a right be set? It seems reasonable to suggest that recognizing a right to begin life with a sound mind and body would require that a child be made better off than he otherwise would be: A fetus with a treatable genetic anomaly, for example, would receive the appropriate medical care so that he could be born unimpaired.[7]

If the right to be born with a sound mind and body is construed to imply a right to be made better off than one otherwise would be, then this right is necessarily a limited one: I can think of no sound reason for recognizing a right to be made beautiful, or a genius, or a star athlete – or even pretty, smart, or strong. The right to be born with a sound mind and body should not be interpreted in terms of perfection (however that is construed), or as implying that the goal of child-bearing is similar to the U.S. Army's promise to help each recruit to 'be all that you can be.' Instead, the right should be more modestly regarded as a right to be as free as possible from significant pain and dysfunction, and this in turn is plausibly interpreted as a right to receive adequate medical care.

The Right to Receive Adequate Medical Care

A good deal of caution must be exercised when basing an argument to require prenatal care on a general right to receive medical care, however, since there is no such legal right recognized in this country at this time: There is no law mandating that medical benefits be offered to everyone, regardless of ability of pay, and the U.S. Supreme Court has ruled that although Congress has opted to subsidize many medically necessary services through various programs, it has no legal obligation to subsidize all medically necessary services [264]. In addition, while federal and state governments support a variety of programs providing health care, they regularly slash their funding – including their funding of those programs aimed at caring for children – with often disastrous results for the ailing individuals [195, 219].

But this may change. There is a new initiative in the U.S. to institute a national health insurance program which would substantially increase access to health care, a movement which even traditional opponents of such programs (such as business corporations and medical associations) are now supporting [76, 114, 165, 185].

One impetus for change is the widespread belief that health care is not merely another commodity, like washing machines and carpets, that instead it has a special importance in our lives that mere commodities do not. The President's Commission for the Study of Ethical Problems in Medicine and Biomedical and Behavioral Research (henceforth,

President's Commission), which documented the persistence and prevalence of this view in America, has argued that the special moral importance of health care creates societal obligations to make it available to everyone:

> Most Americans believe that because health care is special, access to it raises special ethical concerns. In part, this is because good health is by definition important to well-being....In a society concerned not only with fairness and equality of opportunity but also with the redemptive powers of science, there is a felt obligation to ensure that some level of health services is available to all [183, pp. 11-12].

And many people believe that this moral stance should be reinterpreted in the form of a legal right to health care. A 1987 Harris poll, for instance, indicated that over 90 percent of the respondents agreed with the claim that, 'everybody should have the right to get the best possible health care-as good as the treatment a millionaire gets.' Although the scope of a general legal right to health care is a matter of great dispute – whether it should include all desired care or all 'needed' care or be limited to some primary set of health services – there seems to be general agreement that it should in any event include basic prenatal care, which is effective in saving lives and substantially improving health [56, 88, 105, 158, 160, 184].

But it would be unwise to base an analysis of the dilemma at hand on this right, since it is more hypothetical than real. And although access to health care benefits may widen in time, it is not clear that individuals will be considered to have a legal right to this care. Indeed, whether the arguments for a moral right to health care provide adequate justification for a legal right to health care is a matter of debate.[8] This is not to say that ill health should not be prevented when possible, or that claims for a general right to health care should be discounted entirely. Rather, the point is that the controversy concerning proper state intervention with a pregnant woman's activities for the sake of her future child cannot be resolved by appeal to an alleged general right to health care that is itself almost as controversial.

Another interpretation of the right to medical care, however, has more force. According to this interpretation, although there may be no general legal right to medical care enjoyed by everyone, there is a distinctive right to medical care enjoyed by children because of their special vulnerability. In other words, one could argue that children have a moral and legal right to receive basic medical care, and their parents and other caregivers have the corresponding duty to provide that care.

A Child's Right to Medical Care

While parents have a broad moral and legal authority to consent to or refuse medical treatments for their children, this authority is not absolute. Even many supporters of strong parental autonomy recognize that this authority is not the only value, and that human lives should not be sacrificed to it. Thus, although parental authority creates a strong case for noninterference, it is generally agreed that it can justifiably be overridden by considerations of the important interests of children. Indeed, all states recognize as child neglect a parent's refusal to provide adequate medical treatment (although as we shall see, this rule is open to varying interpretations and exceptions).

It could be argued that, in addition, fetuses who will be brought to term should be provided with adequate medical care. The late Michael Bayles [17], for instance, suggests that it should be legally impermissible for a pregnant women to fail to provide a particular medical benefit to a fetus who will be carried to term if failure to provide a similar medical benefit to a born child would be regarded as child neglect or abuse.

While initially plausible, this approach has several serious shortcomings. First, there is no legal consensus on the grounds for legitimate state interference in the case of a parent's failure to provide medical treatment to her children, even in life-and-death cases. While all states recognize as culpable a parent's refusal to allow the administration of life-saving medical treatments to her child, this rule is sometimes breached. One court, for instance, permitted the parents of an institutionalized twelve-year old boy with Down's syndrome to refuse permission for cardiac surgery needed to correct a congenital ventricular septic defect [269], while another permitted the parents of an infant with Down's syndrome to refuse permission for relatively simple corrective surgery needed to join the child's esophagus and stomach [268]. And sometimes the strength of a parent's religious beliefs is determinative: Parents who substitute religious treatment for medical care are protected from criminal liability by exemptions in most state child protection codes (even though failure to seek medical care for other reasons would constitute child neglect), and parents have escaped criminal sanction even when their children died from curable diseases [170, 197].[9]

Yet this exemption is not ironclad, and may be rejected by the courts. Several courts have over-ruled parents' strong religious beliefs by ordering children whose lives were at stake to undergo blood transfusions over the objections of their Jehovah's Witness parents, for instance [170, 197]. And some parents who denied their children life-saving medical care for religious reasons have faced criminal prosecution even in those states with religious exemptions: In Indiana, two couples who were members of the Faith Assembly sect were convicted of reckless homicide and child neglect for the deaths of their infants [170], and a jury in Florida convicted a Christian Science couple of third-degree murder and child abuse for rejecting medical treatment for their daughter in favor of prayer [9].

Courts have sometimes ordered medical treatment over the parent's objections even when the child's condition was not life-threatening.

> Although not commonly, some courts, for example, have prosecuted parents for neglect when their refusal to consent was for treatment that was characterized as 'highly desirable,' though not necessary to save the life of a child. Once declaring the child neglected, courts have, against the religious objections of parents, ordered removal of tonsils, ordered plastic surgery for a massive facial deformity, ordered treatment for emotional ailments, and ordered surgery for a foot deformity [197, pp. 153-154].

In sum, there is no consensus in the law with regard to the circumstances under which parents must provide medical care for their children or face criminal penalties. There are some rules of thumb, however: When a child's life is at stake, the state usually (but not always) requires the parents to seek medical treatment for her; when the child's health is compromised – but her life is not at stake – then the state usually (but not always) allows the parents the discretion to decide.

But even if there were general agreement about when parents must provide medical treatment to their children, we would still be far from resolving the question of what to do with a pregnant woman who refuses medical treatment (and this is the second problem with Bayles' proposal). He is correct to a certain extent: Were there a consensus that the state *may not* intervene in a parent's decision regarding appropriate care of his or her child in certain circumstances, then it would follow that the state would not be justified in intervening in a comparable decision of a pregnant woman regarding her future child as well. But it is important to note that the opposite is not true: Even if there were a consensus that the state may legitimately intervene in a parent's decision regarding her child's medical treatment in certain circumstances, it would not necessarily follow that the state may interfere with the decision of a pregnant woman. For instance, most people would no doubt agree with the assertion by Joseph Goldstein, one of the most ardent supporters of parental authority, that state interference with parental decisions is justifiable when necessary to provide 'any proven, nonexperimental medical procedure when its denial would mean death for a child who would otherwise have an opportunity for either a life worth living or a life of relatively normal healthy growth toward adulthood' [104, p. 162].[10] But while state intervention to prevent the death of a child who might go on to live a full and healthy life seems uncontroversial – at least to those of us who reject the proposition that, if one believes in the power of God, then one must avoid all secular life-saving interventions – we cannot apply this standard directly to the case of a fetus, since (unlike the child) the fetus exists within someone's body. Although the reason for state intervention – saving a life – would be the same in both cases, the justifications for intervention would have to be different, for acting on behalf of an unborn child is more invasive and intrusive to the pregnant woman – insofar as the treatment invades her body – than acting on behalf of the born child would be to a typical parent. In other words, all of the arguments in favor of allowing parents to decide whether and how their children will receive medical treatment are available to pregnant women *plus* one argument that is not usually available to parents in general: the argument that she has a right to decide what will happen to her own body. Hence, standards for a reasonably prudent *pregnant* parent would have to be devised, distinct from standards for reasonably prudent parents in general. (These standards will be discussed later in the chapter and again in Chapters Three and Four.)

There is another shortcoming to resting state intervention to prevent prenatal harm on the future child's alleged right to receive adequate medical care: Since this argument simply holds that (at least) some forms of medical care must be provided, it permits other sorts of harms to go unchallenged. Arguably then, pregnant cigarette smokers who receive periodic medical check-ups and take their prescribed medications would be exempt from interference with their addictions, despite the evidence that smoking during pregnancy may impede fetal growth. For those who wish to be able to protect future persons from all varieties of serious harm, this basis may be too limiting. Thus the alleged right to receive adequate medical care must be buttressed by another right – the general right not to be harmed – in order to include a wide range of prenatal harms.

The Right not to be Harmed

The right not to be harmed is a widely accepted and fundamentally important right which serves as a foundation for our moral and legal codes. Indeed, it is generally accepted in our society that one of the most important goals of state action is to prevent harm to persons, and that this goal may legitimately involve interfering with individual liberty. As the philosopher Joel Feinberg states,

> In short, state interference with a citizen's behavior tends to be morally justified when it is reasonably necessary (that is, when there are reasonable grounds for taking it to be necessary as well as effective) to prevent harm or the unreasonable risk of harm to parties other than the person interfered with. More concisely, the need to prevent harm (private or public) to parties other than the actor is always an appropriate *reason* for legal coercion [82, p. 11].

Some theorists argue that the sole legitimate reason for the state's limiting a person's liberty is to prevent him or her from harming another person. It is significant to note, however, that even if you do not agree that an individual's liberty may be limited only to prevent harm to a third party, you may still believe that the need to prevent harm provides a stronger reason for limiting liberty than any other value.

The right not to be unjustly harmed is even regarded as being enforceable by the state against conduct occurring before birth. The argument for this is one that the tort law recognizes as legitimate: The harm with which we are concerned is suffered by the child after birth, not by the fetus *in utero*.

As Chapter One noted, practically all aspects of a pregnant woman's life take on moral significance because of the potential to harm another person, her future child. There is considerable evidence, for instance, that consuming alcohol, using narcotics, and eating improperly may cause fetal damage; even everyday activities such as drinking coffee and smoking cigarettes may be harmful. A woman who abstains from these activities during pregnancy, however, greatly improves her fetus's health and chances for survival, as does one who alters her lifestyle during pregnancy [12, 49, 64, 135, 176]. Therefore, it makes sense to offer pregnant women information about the effects of lifestyle choices on the outcome of a pregnancy and encourage them to behave differently. The difficult question is whether more should be done. Those who are disturbed by the plight of impaired, low birthweight infants – infants who would have been born healthy had their mothers behaved differently – argue that a pregnant woman should be required to change her lifestyle for the sake of the child she is carrying. The argument is fairly straightforward: By indulging in substance abuse, for instance, the pregnant woman who intends to carry her pregnancy to term is harming another and is thereby violating one of the most fundamental rights of a person, the right not to be harmed; the harm to a woman occasioned by her abstinence would be minor compared with the great benefit to the future child; thus coercing a pregnant woman to alter her lifestyle may be justifiable under some circumstances.

This argument is buttressed by the contention that the state has certain obligations to protect the well-being of individuals, obligations which should be applied equally to all (including newborns). Indeed, one primary obligation of the state is to provide equal protection to all persons. This obligation may be regarded as being grounded in utilitarian concerns (society will benefit most this way) or as being grounded in the principle of equality; the foundational arguments are not really germane here. What is important is that most people would agree that the state does have, and should have, a commitment to the equal protection of all persons.

Arguments Based on a Pregnant Woman's Obligations

Our society is characterized by a high regard for individual rights, and persons on every side of an issue can be expected to couch their arguments in terms of one or more rights. But what are they really talking about? What is a 'right'? What types of beings possess rights? Which rights do they have? Are there rights that outweigh considerations of utility? If so what are these rights? How should we argue for them? What does it mean to say that a right carries a correlative obligation? How should we resolve conflicts among rights? In sum, the issue of rights is an enormously complex and controversial one, and a host of fundamental questions remain open [138, 224, 235].

Because so many issues regarding the scope and power of rights are matters of continuing debate, and some people are thereby unpersuaded by appeals to rights, we need also to consider arguments that avoid references to rights altogether. We have explored one of these so far: the argument based on consequences. Another type of argument is available which also refrains from appealing to the alleged rights of the future child; this one is based on the claim that a pregnant woman has certain obligations to her future child – obligations which may or may not carry correlative rights – and that these obligations are similar to her obligations to other people. While these obligations are not grounded on the rights of the future person, they are related to its interests.

A Pregnant Woman's Moral Obligations to Her Future Child

In the previous chapter it was argued that one's position on the moral status of the fetus has little impact on the issue at hand because there are good arguments for preventing prenatal harms regardless of the moral status of the fetus. These arguments are based on the important interests of the future person (the person the fetus will become if it is brought to term). In essence, the argument is that even if a fetus is not considered to be a person, there still are important interests of a person – the interests of the future child – that must be taken into account. Once a pregnant woman forgoes her right to have an abortion, then, it could be argued that her actions should be constrained by considerations of the welfare of the child that the fetus will become. Her obligations, in other words, would be to the future child, not to the fetus. So even if a pregnant woman has the legal right to have an abortion, it does not follow that she has the freedom to behave in any way she wishes while she is pregnant, for her choices may be limited by considerations of the well-being of the future child.

It follows that a pregnant woman incurs these moral obligations to her future child only if she intends to carry the fetus to term. If a woman is free to terminate her pregnancy but does not do so, then she has chosen not to avoid a situation in which she and she alone can affect the well-being of another person (the child she will bear), and in so choosing she can be deemed to have assumed responsibility for the condition of that future person. And, it could be argued, society should recognize these moral obligations to be legal obligations as well, backed by the coercive power of the state. Although it is not always desirable to recognize moral duties as legal duties, one area in which moral responsibility and legal responsibility coincide pertains to what the noted legal scholar H.L.A. Hart calls a person's 'role-responsibility':

> A sea captain is responsible for the safety of his ship, and that is his responsibility, or one of his responsibilities. A husband is responsible for the maintenance of his wife; perhaps for the upbringing of their children; a sentry for alerting the guard at the enemy's approach....These examples of a person's responsibilities suggest the generalization that, whenever a person occupies a distinctive place or office in a social organization, to which specific duties are attached to provide for the welfare of others or to advance in some specific way the aims or purposes of the organization, he is properly said to be responsible for the performance of these duties, or for doing what is necessary to fulfill them [109, p. 242].

It could be argued that part of the 'role-responsibility' of a pregnant woman is to provide for the welfare of the child she will bear.[11]

Discussion

So far we have argued that there are sound reasons – reasons based on utilitarian considerations, the rights of future persons, and the moral obligations of pregnant women – for holding that a woman should not be free to do whatever she wishes with her body while she is pregnant. This implies that there are *some* circumstances under which it would be legitimate to coerce a pregnant woman to act in the interests of her child-to-be. But what are these circumstances? And what sorts of coercion would be appropriate?

At this stage of our investigation, any answer to these questions would be premature; we must first analyze the nature of a woman's (proposed) legal obligations (including the counter-arguments to recognizing any legal duty on a woman's part to her future child) before we can come to any conclusions. This complicated process begins in this chapter, proceeds through the next chapter's examination of countervailing considerations and into Chapter Four's discussion of concrete cases.

Preliminary Remarks on the Nature of a Pregnant Woman's Legal Obligations to Act in the Interests of her Child-to-be

A parent's legal duties towards his or her child are based in large part on the interests of the child, but they are limited by the interests and rights of others (including those of the parent herself). Thus a parent is not obligated to do what is in the child's best interest, but rather the parent must act within some acceptable range of these interests, a 'range of reasonableness' [230]. This range is necessarily flexible, given the economic and social variances (and inequities) across society, the range of values and beliefs within society, and the broad scope of a typical parent's responsibilities: to her other children, her spouse, her employer, herself. In application, then, this standard may be very similar to a 'minimum needs' standard, which holds that a parent must satisfy at least certain minimum needs of his or her child. Should a parent fall below this range, creating significant risk of serious and long-lasting harm to his or her child, then the state may step in to protect the child. The California Supreme Court has proposed that the fundamental question to be asked in these cases is: 'What would an ordinarily reasonable and prudent parent have done in similar circumstances?' [259].

Society could also recognize a flexible standard of due care on the part of a pregnant woman with regard to the child she will bear. This legal standard of care would involve refraining from acts which a reasonably prudent pregnant person would avoid when that person knows or, in the exercise of reasonable care, should know that such acts cause prenatal harm. The pregnant woman's duty would also extend to the provision of those benefits (such as some forms of medical treatment) that a reasonably careful pregnant person would provide. Using such standards would allow a woman to engage in risky conduct which the reasonably prudent pregnant person would pursue, and would allow her to act in ways that cause relatively minor prenatal harms [215].

One objection to this formula is that, when it comes to a woman's actions during pregnancy, 'reasonableness' is simply not a reliable standard. As one commentator worries,

> Given common stereotypical public concepts of the 'proper' role of women, particularly pregnant women, there is very little behavior that might not be found by a jury to be 'unreasonable.' This is particularly a risk when juries are confronted with injuries that will otherwise go unremedied, as is likely often to be true in such cases. It would not, in fact, be 'unreasonable' for a pregnant woman, faced with the prospect of post-natal civil liability according to community standards of propriety, to assume that the only safe course of behavior is to lie prone for nine months [118, p. 616, n. 68].

But this assumption is unwarranted. The reasonableness standard is not an ideal of perfection to which pregnant women should aspire; it does not require that a woman give up her whole life, or even a large part of her life, to her pregnancy. Indeed, the point of setting a flexible standard of reasonableness – a standard that varies according to community mores, access to medical care, the level of medical technology available, the stage of the pregnancy, and so on – is to posit a minimum standard below which one cannot fall without being viewed as culpably negligent. Thus although a pregnant woman is not expected to do everything in her power to ensure a healthy baby (such as staying in bed for nine months), she is expected to show at least a modicum of due care for the well-being of her future child.

It seems plausible to contend that the standard of care would involve two distinct levels of obligation. The woman assumes the first one by becoming pregnant, regardless of whether she does so voluntarily or not.[12] While she is pregnant, the possibility remains that a child will come into being, who will be affected by her actions, so she has at least some level of obligation of due care to this future person. The pregnant woman assumes the second level of obligation by forgoing her right to have an abortion for any reason other than jeopardy to her life and/or health, and hence at least tacitly committing herself to carrying the fetus to term. Once she makes this decision, or at least allows the fetus to reach the point at which abortions are permitted only to mitigate risks to maternal life and/or health, she puts herself in a special relationship to her future child. This relationship can be seen as carrying more demanding obligations, obligations which are similar to those of any parent to his or her child.

It is generally held that the parent-child relationship involves positive duties of aid as well as negative duties not to cause harm, and parents are expected to sacrifice more for their children than they would for strangers. At this later stage of pregnancy, then, a woman may be required to undergo more than minimally invasive therapies in order to prevent serious harm to her child-to-be, and she may be required to accept significant limitations on her freedom of action in order not to cause harm. But there are good reasons for positing that a pregnant woman's obligations at the earlier stage, the first level of obligation, should be substantially less burdensome.

First Level of Legal Obligation

Women become pregnant for a variety of reasons that have nothing to do with the desire to have a child: They are raped, their method of contraception fails, they take inadequate precautions against getting pregnant, and so on. But whatever the circumstances of conception, it is often true that a pregnancy is unintended and unwelcome. Thus we should be hesitant about presuming that all pregnant women regard themselves as parents; and we should be hesitant about adding too many extra burdens – in the form of legal obligations to undergo invasive medical treatments or difficult lifestyle changes – on a woman whose pregnancy may already be burdensome to her and who retains the option of having an abortion.

Given these considerations, it would make sense to understand a woman's legal obligations during the early stage of pregnancy as similar to the duty of due care she owes to any other person (e.g., any stranger), which is relatively undemanding. According to commonsense morality and most ethical theories, one has a general, though limited, duty of care toward strangers, independent of any voluntary assumption of responsibility for their welfare.

One strong case for a discretionless duty to aid a stranger is offered by James Childress (drawing on Eric D'Arcy's work):

> A has a duty of beneficence to do X for P: 1) when P is at risk of significant loss or damage (such as severe injury or death), 2) when A's action is necessary to prevent this loss or damage, 3) when A's action would probably prevent it, 4) when the likely harms to A are minimal, and 5) when the benefit that P will probably gain outweighs the likely harm to A [41, p. 31; 63].

If we substitute 'future person' for 'P' and 'pregnant woman' for 'A' in Childress's example, we can see that all of his conditions may pertain to the cases at hand. The pregnant woman may choose to end her obligations by having an abortion (a subject which will be addressed further in the next chapter).

Legal Obligations to Strangers

The backbone of our legal system is the conviction that one person should not harm another. There is, in other words, a generally recognized legal duty to refrain from harming another person, a duty whose strength is not diminished when strangers are involved. Hence the law extracts monetary damages and in some situations imposes criminal penalties upon those who cause harm to others through negligent, reckless or willful conduct.

It could be argued that many activities of pregnant women fall under this rubric. A pregnant woman who ingests crack, for instance, could be said to show reckless disregard for the risk of harm which her conduct poses for the child she intends to bear. And a pregnant woman who negligently causes an automobile accident which injures her fetus could reasonably be accused of misconduct with regard to her future child. It would be a fairly straightforward task, then, to apply the principles of some legal prohibitions against harming others to pregnant women who cause prenatal damage.

But we are also interested in those instances in which the pregnant woman does not directly cause harm to her future child but instead refuses to prevent a harm from occurring; in other words, she fails to take action to avoid the harm. One example of this would be a pregnant woman who refuses to take a prescribed medicine which would ameliorate a genetic anomaly in her fetus; another would be a woman who refuses the cesarean section needed to save her distressed fetus. The issue here is whether a pregnant woman should ever be legally obligated to come to the aid of her future child, in addition to being legally obligated to refrain from harming him or her.

The proposal that the courts should recognize that a pregnant woman has a limited obligation to prevent serious harm to her future child even in the early stages of pregnancy is consonant with many legal systems: Czechoslovakia, France, Germany, Hungary, Italy, The Netherlands, Norway, Poland, Portugal, Rumania, U.S.S.R., and Turkey have statutes that create a general duty to rescue (so long as the risk to the rescuer is minimal). But it seems to founder when we confront the reality of Anglo-American law, which generally assumes and imports that there is no legal duty to aid a stranger [132, 182]. I may notice that a stranger is about to walk into a deep pit because he is completely absorbed in looking at a rainbow, and at very little inconvenience to me, simply by giving a shout, I could save him from serious harm. But I do not. I simply watch him continue to walk while he admires the rainbow, until, with a shriek, he falls into the pit. Does the law hold me liable for his harm? No. Does the law claim that I should have aided him? No. Does the law pay any attention to me at all? No.

Indeed, Anglo-American law has not deigned to notice a horrifying list of one person's failure to aid another:

> The common-law tradition has left unpunished even harmful omissions of an immoral kind – malicious failures to warn a blind man of an open manhole, to lift the head of a sleeping drunk out of a puddle of water, to throw a rope from a bridge to a drowning swimmer, to rescue or even report the discovery of a small child wandering lost in a wood, and so on. Not only negligent but wicked samaritans

> have escaped answerability to the law, which in English-speaking countries has not only declined to punish them, but has not even made them liable for damages to those they have failed to aid [82, p. 127].

If according to our legal tradition a person need not take the smallest trouble to prevent serious harm to a stranger, is there any basis for claiming that a pregnant woman should be held legally accountable for failing to aid the child she may (or may not) bear?

Were this the whole story, it would seem unfair to hold pregnant women to standards that are applied to no one else.[13] But the situation is a bit more complicated. The first point to be noted is that the strength of the assumption that there is no legal duty to aid a stranger seems to be waning: Several states (Alaska, Minnesota, Vermont, Rhode Island and Massachusetts) have passed statutes delineating those (limited) circumstances in which people are required to aid strangers in distress,[14] and courts are increasingly recognizing exceptions to the rule.[15] But more importantly, it is reasonable to argue that the objections usually raised against positing a legally enforceable duty to aid are not relevant to the cases at hand.

The most common challenge to establishing a legal duty to aid strangers in peril is that it would interfere too much with an individual's liberty and welfare, either because the sacrifice in an particular instance would be too great or because the small sacrifices required to aid the large numbers of people who require assistance would inevitably become overwhelming. However, both of these objections fail when applied to pregnant women.

First, only minimal sacrifices on the pregnant woman's part would be required at this stage – undergoing relatively risk-free and proven forms of therapy, such as inoculations or doses of safe medications – and these need not be any more onerous than state regulations of other activities. As John Robertson [190, pp. 359-360] points out, 'Compelling certain diagnostic tests or even medications is not materially different from fluoridation or compulsory vaccinations.'[16] The second reason the typical objections to an enforceable duty to aid a stranger fail in these cases is that compelling a pregnant woman to prevent harm to her future child is not at all likely to result in further impositions on her to aid a large number of other strangers: It is easy to distinguish precisely who she is expected to aid (the being inside her) from all other persons in need of assistance of some sort.

A different type of objection to imposing a general legal duty to aid a stranger is based on the idea that it is difficult, if not impossible, to determine which individual is required to come to the aid of a particular stranger. Since strangers are in no special relationship to one another, in principle there are many potential benefactors for anyone in need. And in any given instance, there will most likely be several people who could come to the aid of a particular person, yet each of them might refrain from acting on the reasonable assumption that one of the others, perhaps one who is more able, would assist the stranger. Given this, the argument continues, it is unfair to single out one person and charge him or her with failing to aid a particular stranger in peril.

This objection, however, simply has no force in the situations under discussion here. Since the harm to be prevented is harm to a future person – who now exists within the woman's body – there is no one else who could act instead of the pregnant woman. Thus it would not do to say that it is unfair to single her out among an indefinitely large number of possible benefactors, since she is the only possible benefactor.

We may conclude, then, that the usual arguments against holding one stranger legally responsible for helping another have very little force when applied to pregnant women.[17] Hence we are well on our way to being able to contend with confidence that a pregnant woman may have legal obligations to refrain from causing harm and also to take steps to prevent harm to her future child, even at the beginning of a pregnancy, so long as these obligations impose no significant burdens on her. But we are not yet there, for the countervailing considerations have yet to be addressed.

Determining When a Pregnant Woman's Legal Obligations to her Future Child Become More Stringent

The second level of obligation – the more demanding duties owed to one's own child – does not come into force until it is clear that the pregnant woman will go to term. This may or may not be a matter of choice on her part; a pregnant woman need not voluntarily accept a special relationship with her future child in order to be treated as having assumed responsibility for its well-being. The rationale for this position begins with a brief examination of the power of the state to limit a woman's right to seek an abortion.

In 1973, the Supreme Court ruled in *Roe v. Wade* [293] that a pregnant woman has a legal right to seek an abortion, but that her freedom to do so changed throughout her pregnancy. The Court held that, as a woman's pregnancy advanced, so did the state's power to regulate abortions, and the Court delineated three stages at which the level of state control may change. During the first stage of pregnancy, roughly the first trimester, the Court ruled that a woman may seek an abortion for any reason, free from all state intervention other than the requirement that the procedure be performed by a licensed physician. After the first trimester, the state may choose to regulate the abortion procedure 'in ways that are reasonably related to maternal health.' During the third stage – when the fetus is viable – the state's interest in protecting potential human life is strengthened considerably, and the Court ruled that the state may go so far as to proscribe abortion 'except where it is necessary, in appropriate medical judgment, for the preservation of the life or health of the mother' [293].

Since that time abortion procedures have become considerably safer, and in 1983 the Supreme Court ruled that many of the second trimester restrictions placed on abortion procedures ten years earlier were no longer necessary [252]. In effect, then, the Court collapsed the original three stages of pregnancy into two. During the first stage – which begins at conception and proceeds until the fetus is able to survive outside its mother's body (the point of 'fetal viability') – the state has little control to limit abortions. After the fetus is viable, however, the state's power to intervene is strong, and it can go so far as to prohibit all abortions except for those needed to save the life or health of the mother.

Consequently, there is now one major point, fetal viability, which designates when the state may intrude into a woman's decision to seek an abortion. It is important to note, however, that viability may not continue to be that point, since it is an arbitrary and shifting criterion, posing an enormous number of legal and ethical problems [95, 187]. One major difficulty is that the point of 'viability' may be different for each fetus, since it depends upon, among other factors, maternal health, fetal weight, gestational age, genetic composition, and available medical care.[18] Hence the notion of fetal viability is rarely used in areas of the law not pertaining to abortion. The Rhode Island Supreme Court, for instance, concluded that,

> If we profess allegiance to reason, it would be seditious to adopt so arbitrary and uncertain a concept as viability as a dividing line between those persons who shall enjoy the protection of our remedial laws and those who shall become, for most intents and purposes, nonentities [287].

In its 1989 decision in *Webster v. Reproductive Health Services* [307], the Supreme Court indicated its willingness to abandon the trimester analysis in general and the emphasis on fetal viability in particular. It will be years before the issues are resolved in all states, but a good guess is that viability as a major criterion will be discarded, and a more secure line of demarcation will be drawn between a woman's unqualified right to seek an abortion and the state's authority to curtail that right. But no doubt there will continue to be some line of demarcation between the stage at which a pregnant woman may seek an abortion for any reason and the stage at which the state may limit her choices. The relevance of this to our discussion is that, before any line of demarcation has been reached, a pregnant woman cannot be said to have committed herself to carrying the pregnancy to term, since she may seek an abortion for any reason. After that time has passed, however, and the state permits her to seek an abortion only under certain conditions (such as endangerment to her life or health), we may reasonably assume that she will continue the pregnancy to term. In sum, it makes sense to conclude that a pregnant woman does not incur the second, more stringent level of obligation to her future child until it is uncontroversially the case that she intends to carry the pregnancy to term, and this would not be until she has forgone her legal right to seek an abortion for reasons other than risk to her life or health. Thus she would have no legal obligation to undergo any significant burdens for the sake of her future child before that time.

State Intervention

So far we have explored arguments in favor of recognizing that a woman has some legal obligations to act in the interests of her future child. But other factors must be considered to determine whether or not legal coercion may be allowed. Among the most important of these are the Fourteenth Amendment's requirements of due process of law and equal protection of the law.

Requirements of Due Process

Due process of law is a constitutional guarantee of fundamental fairness, an affirmation of respect for those liberties which, as the Supreme Court stated, are 'so rooted in the traditions and conscience of our people as to be ranked as fundamental' [299]. Due process requirements are designed to assure that the rights and interests at stake are respected, and to avoid abuses and errors in the state's decision to intervene. Before pregnant women could be held to particular standards of behavior, these standards would have to be authorized by statute or developed through court-created common law and widely promulgated. To prevent the woman who is the party in a precedent-setting case from being subjected to the newly created common law (about which she could have had no warning), the judge should have the discretion to make his or her decision completely non-retroactive: Thus, only future parties would be subjected to the new common law's coercion. In addition, judicial review of the decision to intervene should be available.

Unfortunately, physicians have not always acted in accordance with even the most minimal requirements of due process. A case was reported in 1984, for instance, in which physicians performed a cesarean section on a pregnant woman in order to save an acutely distressed term fetus, even though the woman continually and 'adamantly' refused to give consent to the surgery and even though a court order had not been secured [121]. This is tantamount to assault and battery. A physician is not justified in interfering with a pregnant woman's decision simply because it is detrimental to the welfare of her child-to-be. Instead, the physician must go through regular institutional channels such as the courts. It is important to note, however, that seeking judicial review is not always sufficient to meet the requirements of due process, as Chapter Four will demonstrate.

The Fourteenth Amendment also guarantees that states afford equal protection of the law to all persons who are 'similarly situated'. Some commentators have interpreted this to mean that it is wrong to place legal constraints on pregnant women that are not also placed on men and nonpregnant women. But this conclusion is too strong. There may be circumstances in which a class of pregnant women, with their unique needs and responsibilities, can be rationalized as appropriately separate from women generally. In these cases, state regulation of pregnant women may be necessary without having to regulate all women or all persons. At least in principle, then, some state intervention into the activities of pregnant women may be constitutional [86, 191]; this topic will be analyzed further in the next chapter.

Proportionality

Although the factor motivating state intervention in the lives of pregnant women is the prevention of serious harm to future persons, it does not follow that the appropriate social policy would be to interfere in every instance in which a pregnant woman is posing significant harm to her future child. Administering such a program would no doubt prove unworkable: inefficient, awkward and unreasonably intrusive. Other factors must also be considered, especially proportionality: The intervention should not create more harm than it is aimed to alleviate. Allowing legal interference in every instance in which a future child is or could be harmed might create more harm than good, and thereby would defeat the whole point of intervening. This stands as a powerful reason for limiting state intervention. It also leads us to conclude that state interference would be justifiable only if four conditions can be met: 1) The harms to be prevented to the future person greatly exceed the degree of invasion to the pregnant woman, 2) the intervention is expected to be successful, 3) the intervention involves the least intrusive means available, and 4) a policy permitting such interventions will be, on the whole, beneficial to society in general. A few words on the first two conditions are in order here; the others will be discussed in later chapters.

Weighing Particular Harms and Benefits

Determining whether the harms to be prevented to the future person in fact greatly exceed the degree of invasion to the pregnant woman is not an easy task, and involves weighing three interrelated factors: magnitude of harm, probability that the harm will occur, and probability that the harm can be prevented or removed. No simple formula for the application of these factors in all situations exists; at best, one can give a general outline of their scope and relevance [150].

The question of the magnitude of the harms involved has two parts: 1) To what extent will the future child be harmed by his mother's actions? and 2) to what extent will the pregnant woman be harmed if her decision is overruled and her body is invaded? Answering these questions requires determining which interests are at stake (e.g., a woman's interest in making her own decisions, a child's interest in not being disabled), and the degree to which each interest will be invaded (a matter of duration times severity). One interest at stake, for instance, would be the woman's interest in bodily integrity, and different actions would invade it to different degrees: The extent of harm to this interest caused by a mandatory inoculation is substantially less than that caused by a forced cesarean section. Since it makes a difference how important the interest is and whether it is being only slightly thwarted or down-right defeated, these two actions would require different types of justification [82].

Determining the probability that the pregnant woman's actions will in fact cause grave harm to her future child is also an important and troublesome factor. There should be ample evidence to indicate that there is a high probability of serious harm to the future child if steps are not taken to intervene on its behalf, but this certainty is often lacking. For instance, the probability of the risk of harm is especially difficult to determine in instances of environmental or workplace hazards because many of the harms in question have a multitude of contributing causes and often are the result of cumulative or synergistic influences. And although we may have significant evidence that drinking alcohol during pregnancy may cause serious prenatal harm, for example, there is no evidence that this is always the case. Hence it is often difficult in any particular instance to determine with certainty whether or not the future child is at grave risk of serious harm.

The third factor to be considered is the probability that the harm to the future child can be avoided or removed. Intervention makes sense only when there is a significant or high probability that a harm can be prevented or at least ameliorated. One is obligated neither to make futile efforts to prevent harm, nor to suffer especially risky or experimental measures. The central question is easily discerned: What constitutes a 'significant' probability that intervention will be successful?

With respect to fetal therapies, the answer involves three factors: 1) the general reliability of this type of therapy as determined by prevailing standards of the medical profession; 2) its estimated efficacy in this instance; and 3) the value of the expected results (for example, the value of a generally healthy life or of a brief life filled with great pain).

It is appropriate to allow the pregnant woman the discretion to choose any of various treatment options when the proposed medical care is a matter of debate within the medical community and there is no medical consensus regarding the appropriate treatment for the child. The difficult questions regarding the scope of her discretion do not concern a choice among ordinary therapies but rather involve a decision to reject them entirely, or to forgo a less-than-satisfactory conventional therapy in favor of a promising but unorthodox one. This issue cannot be decided in isolation from the other interests mentioned, but it does point to the importance of one factor: the value of the expected results. It makes a difference whether the treatment can be expected to cure the child, to mitigate the symptoms without curing, or to save the child's life but leave her in a permanently comatose state. The general principle is intuitive: The obligation of a parent to utilize a particular therapy decreases in direct proportion with the tentativeness of the desired results of that therapy.

The problem of determining the scope and limits of the obligation to provide 'effective' therapy is not a problem unique to fetal therapy: It is present throughout medicine. Reflection on this factor, however, does lead to the conclusion that social and legal policy must be selective. To assert that no fetal therapy should be mandated, or that all should be, would be unreasonable. Different therapies promise different outcomes, and only those that are likely to be effective in avoiding or ameliorating severely deleterious conditions may be required. The final decision, of course, cannot be made without balancing the severity of the harm to the future child against the risk to the pregnant woman of intervening.

Preliminary Conclusions

So far, this chapter has argued that there are good moral and prudential reasons for trying to prevent prenatal harms, reasons based on three types of considerations: 1) utility (i.e., more good than harm will result), 2) the future person's positive right to receive adequate medical care and his negative right not to be harmed; and 3) the pregnant woman's general obligations to refrain from harming another and to aid another, as well as her special obligation to care for her future child. In other words, it makes good moral sense to argue that a pregnant woman does not have *carte blanche* to act any way she wishes, at least if her actions will cause harm to her future child. In addition, this chapter has contended that it may be justifiable for the state to intervene to prevent some prenatal harms, but that there are two important factors which ought to be taken into account before doing so: due process and proportionality.

While there may be good arguments in favor of limiting the liberty of pregnant women in order to protect their offspring, these arguments are far from justifying any and all types of state intervention. First is the practical matter of proportionality: Allowing the state to interfere in every instance in which a future child is or could be harmed would no doubt create more harm than good, and this stands as a powerful reason for limiting state intervention. And second, we have argued that there are two distinct levels of obligation to which pregnant women may be held – the first involves minor duties of due care, while the second level involves more stringent duties similar to those in a parent-child relationship – and that the burdens a pregnant woman may be expected to bear grow as the pregnancy advances. The implications of this for state intervention are profound: The state would not be justified in intervening to prevent some very troubling prenatal harms simply because they are caused during the early stage of pregnancy and dealing with them would place an unwarranted burden on the pregnant woman.

The discussion so far has been fairly abstract, and necessarily so. We cannot make reasonable conclusions about concrete cases until all of the relevant moral, legal, and public policy issues have been addressed. And so far we have considered only a small subset of those arguments that bear on the issue at hand: Only the arguments in favor of coercing a pregnant woman to behave in certain ways have been advanced. We have been looking, in other words, at the rights of the future child, the duties of the pregnant woman to the future child, and possible benefits – to the children and to society in general – of preventing prenatal harms. But there are many other arguments to examine before a final determination can be made. We must, for instance, consider a pregnant woman's duties in conjunction with her rights and liberties, and we must examine other sorts of factors that militate against state intervention in these cases, such as the disbenefits that might result.

Thus although the thrust of the discussion so far has been that it is reasonable to impose some legal limitations on the choices open to pregnant women, these conclusions are only preliminary because other important relevant ingredients have yet to be taken into account. The arguments against state intervention into the lives of pregnant women, which will be examined in the next chapter, are at least as strong as the arguments in favor of state intervention.

Notes

[1] As Justice Cardozo stated in a now-famous decision, 'Every human being of adult years and sound mind has a right to determine what shall be done with his own body; and a

surgeon who performs an operation without his patient's consent commits an assault, for which he is liable in damages' [295]. For more on this subject, see [78].

[2] The National Commission to Prevent Infant Mortality estimates that, for every low birthweight prevented, the general health care system would save between $14,000 and $30,000 [67].

[3] The National Commission to Prevent Infant Mortality estimates that if the 1985 U.S. mortality rate had been 5.5 per 1000 births (instead of 10.6 per 1000 births), and if the number of low birthweight infants had been reduced by half, an additional $6.4 billion to $12 billion would have been earned over the children's lifetime – approximately $1.4 billion to $2.6 billion of which would have been paid in taxes [67].

[4] Since we assume nothing about the moral status of the fetus, and are acquiescing to the legal principle that the fetus has no legally protectable interests, it follows that the fetus has no rights strong enough to outweigh its mother's rights.

[5] It should be noted, however, that these rights do not necessarily imply that there is also a right to be born. The duty to provide medical treatment, for example, to the fetus who will be carried to term is a duty to the post-fetal person she will become *if* she is carried to term, and it need not entail a duty to carry her to term.

[6] While 'the right to begin life with a sound mind and body' has been adopted by other courts [267, 310] the right of a child to be born as a 'whole, functional human being' has held little sway, and indeed was rejected almost immediately by the New York Court of Appeals [246].

[7] There is another possible interpretation of this right: that a child who cannot be born healthy may have the right not to be born at all.

Consider the following hypothetical case. Diagnostic procedures performed on Mrs. D. reveal that the fetus she is carrying is severely impaired: the fetus has spina bifida (an open spinal column), hydrocephalus (excess fluid on the brain), microcephaly (an abnormally small head and brain), and an improperly formed brain stem. Although it is anticipated that the child will survive past infancy, it is clear that he cannot be born with, and will never enjoy, 'a sound mind and body,' nor will he ever be a 'whole, functioning human being.' If the child has a right to be born sound and whole, and this right cannot be met, does it follow that he has a right not to be born at all?

The existence of such a right would have profound effects. If a child has a right to begin life with a sound mind and body, then any action which interferes with that right would be *prima facie* wrongful, even if the action does not worsen the condition of the child. This means that bringing an impaired child into the world – even if it is not possible under the circumstances to produce a healthy child – would be wrong, since it violates his right to be born healthy. Some commentators have argued for such a position, and have suggested that legislators at least consider prohibiting certain acts by pregnant women: exposing a fetus to 'the mother's defective intrauterine environment caused by her genotype,' for instance, and carrying a seriously defective child to term [209].

There are several ways for the state to recognize this right. One method of protecting a right not to be born unhealthy is to monitor all potential parents and refuse to permit those individuals who are likely to pass on severely deleterious genes to reproduce. We could, in other words, create a legal duty to refrain from passing on certain genes [208]. The state could screen all men and women of child-bearing age: Those who are fertile and who are at high risk of having seriously impaired children could be sterilized.

A second method of protecting the right not to be born would be to monitor all pregnant women and to require those who are carrying severely impaired fetuses to obtain abortions. This would mean compelling some pregnant women to get abortions against their wills and against their most fundamental beliefs.

Another alternative is to utilize the tort law: The child could be allowed to sue for compensation for having been born severely impaired, or someone could sue on the child's behalf. Courts have been confronted with the difficult task of addressing these suits – usually referred to as 'wrongful life' cases – since the early 1960s (See Chapter Four, Note 25). In a wrongful life suit, the child argues that her being born with serious impairments (even though there was no possibility that she could be born without the impairments) was a harm that calls for compensation, and she claims damages for having to live with her permanent and severe handicaps. In a way, the child claims that her suffering is so great that it would have been better had she not been born.

And finally, infanticide could be legalized. Infanticide is an option insofar as the desire to prevent prenatal harms is motivated by the desire to reduce human suffering, and one way to reduce human suffering is to eliminate the people who suffer the most. Infanticide for any reason at all is not the issue here; we are considering infanticide as a means of mitigating human suffering in the same way we are considering state intervention into the lives of pregnant women to prevent prenatal harms as a means of mitigating human suffering. In other words, infanticide may be considered to be an alternative means of dealing with devastatingly severe prenatal harms, and it offers the potential for reducing the suffering occasioned by some prenatal harms without intruding on the autonomy of pregnant women.

While theoretically plausible, none of these alternatives offers a viable solution to the dilemma at hand. Most courts continue to reject wrongful life suits, for instance, and states are increasingly moving to prohibit them by statute. And given the serious shortcomings of the other proposals – the invasions of privacy, the overtones of prejudice, the negation of individual liberty, the assault on self-determination, the lack of respect for human life, the unacceptable increase of state control, and the inevitable abuse of such discretionary power – these options are likely to be anathema to most people. They are not being recommended here.

[8] Although this is not the place to give a comprehensive survey of the complex debate over the existence of a right to health care, a few comments on two basic methods for arguing for the general right are in order. We can reject immediately the method that relies upon any naturalistic assertions, such as the claim that one has a right to receive health care because one has a need for health care. Ever since the eighteenth century, when David Hume argued that value judgments cannot be deduced from a statement of fact without an intervening nonfactual value premise, such inferences have been discredited. Moreover, needing something – en needing it desperately – is not the same as having a right to it. And recognizing a personal moral obligation to respond to a need is not the same as recognizing a legal duty of the state to respond to that need.

A different, more plausible method is to derive the right to health care from the existence of other rights. The argument would be as follows: One has a certain set of political rights (e.g., the right to free speech and the right to vote), and in order to exercise these rights, one needs a certain set of basic goods (such as decent health); since everyone has these political rights, everyone should also have the means of exercising them, and the means should be provided to them as a matter of right; since one needs medical care in order to have good health, one also should have the right to medical care. This argument, however, does not really work: The recognition of a political right does not require the state to correct any natural condition that prevents the exercise of that right.

[9] These exemptions are based on the U.S. Constitution's First Amendment's guarantee of free exercise of religion.

[10] Although most people might agree with this statement, not all would: Members of religious sects who believe in faith healing rather than secular methods of medical care would find this conclusion highly objectionable. Their concerns will be addressed in Chapter Four.

[11] Consider the following case. Arthur is the public health director for the state of –. It has come to his attention that a certain underground well is contaminated, but he neglects to publicize the fact or to inform the authorities in the area. So people continue to drink the poisoned water, and many become very ill. Here Arthur has had nothing to do with the poisoning of the well, nor does he influence people to drink from it. He simply sits at his desk and works on other matters. Thus we could give an adequate causal explanation of the poisonings without mentioning Arthur. Yet although he did not cause the harm, he still is to a certain degree responsible for it – both morally and legally – since, as part of his position as public health director, he had a duty to prevent people from drinking the contaminated water. In the same way, a pregnant woman may be responsible – both morally and legally – for the impaired health of the child she bears.

[12] Commentators have paid a good deal of attention to the issue of the moral implications of a woman's responsibility for becoming pregnant. For instance, one important question is: If the fetus were considered to be a person, would a pregnant woman's obligations to it depend on whether or not she was responsible for becoming pregnant?

There have been varying responses to this question. In a well-known article, Judith Jarvis Thomson posits that a pregnant woman's obligations to her fetus does depend in large part on her degree of voluntariness in becoming pregnant. Thomson argues, for instance, that a woman who becomes pregnant as the result of a rape would have no obligations to the fetus, while a woman who simply did not bother to take precautions would [228]. On the other hand, Holly Smith argues that even if a woman voluntarily becomes pregnant, she still may not be obligated to continue the pregnancy [217].

While interesting and important, these arguments over the moral weight of a woman's responsibility for becoming pregnant are irrelevant to the issue of her responsibility for causing prenatal harm. There are several reasons for this, and a brief discussion of them might help to clarify the issues at hand. First, the debate over the weight to be given to a woman's role in becoming pregnant – whether or not it limits the strength of her obligations to the fetus – makes sense only if the fetus is assumed to be a person. But we are making no such assumption here. Rather, we are assuming that the fetus is not a person, and the thrust of the discussion is to analyze the contention that, even if the fetus is not a person, there still are important interests of a person (the future child) which must be weighed against those of the pregnant woman (and the interests of the future person do not become significant until its mother has decided to carry it to term).

The second point is that the argument between Thomson and Smith is an argument regarding the legitimacy of abortion. Their concern is to address the issue of whether it would be ethically acceptable for a woman to have an abortion even if she did nothing to avoid getting pregnant. I, of course, am not taking a stand on the moral legitimacy of abortion in any particular circumstances. Instead, I am accepting the legal fact that a woman in this country may seek an abortion for any reason (at least during the first few months of pregnancy), and I am proceeding from there.

The point of my investigation – in contrast to the argument between Thomson and Smith – is to address the question: Even though a woman has the right to seek an abortion, and even though the fetus is not a person, does a pregnant woman still have some obligations to refrain from harming the fetus? And I am answering this question by appealing to the important interests of the child the fetus will become if it is carried to term. The degree of voluntariness on the part of a woman in becoming pregnant plays no significant role in this context (so long as she has the option of terminating the pregnancy); what matters is whether or not she intends to continue the pregnancy and bear the child.

[13] And this is precisely what some commentators conclude [187].

[14] Laws requiring one stranger to aid another who is in distress are generally known as 'Bad Samaritan' laws. They are to be distinguished from the more widely adopted 'Good Samaritan' laws, which do not impose a duty to rescue but instead shield the rescuer (usually a health care professional) from legal liability should he harm the accident victim he is attempting to help.

[15] Courts have recognized a variety of relationships between strangers – carrier and passenger, employer and employee, uninjured automobile accident victim and injured victim – that warrant one to aid the other [132, 182]. See, for instance, [257, 304].

The U.S. Congress decided to establish a different sort of obligation to aid. The 1986 Consolidated Omnibus Budget Reconciliation Act (42 U.S.C. 1395dd) requires hospitals with emergency services that participate in the Medicare program to stabilize all emergency cases and all women in active labor before transferring or discharging them.

[16] While fluoridation may not be an apt example, since in most places nonfluoridated water is available for purchase by people who wish to reduce their intake of fluoridated water, Robertson's general point is nonetheless well-taken.

[17] It is important to note as well that there are many cogent arguments in favor of a general legal duty to aid a stranger in distress [82, 115, 132, 234].

[18] Since the Court's ruling in *Roe v. Wade* [293], there has been considerable discussion about what 'fetal viability' really means: When precisely is a fetus viable? The Supreme Court decided not to decide this question. In *Planned Parenthood of Central Missouri V. Danforth* [286], for instance, the Court stated that it is not the 'proper function of the legislature or the courts to place viability, which essentially is a medical concept, at a specific point in the gestation period...the determination of whether a particular fetus is viable is, and must be, a matter for the judgment of the responsible attending physician.' In a later case, the Court reiterated its position, noting that there is no general community standard of viability and that it must be decided on a case-by-case basis [253]. The Court thus gave broad discretion to physicians in making their decisions.

In one sense, this was a very reasonable stance for the Court to take. If viability as a criterion is inexact and shifting, then so be it. It is much better for physicians, who keep pace with new medical developments, to decide when a particular fetus is viable than for courts of law or legislative bodies to attempt this onerous task. Yet in a way this discretion is burdensome for physicians and their patients, who seek assurance through legal guidelines. In fact, health care providers often set their own straightforward and arbitrary limits on performing abortions. Even before the Supreme Court's 1989 ruling in *Webster v.*

Reproductive Health Services [307] many physicians would not abort a fetus who had gestated for twenty weeks or more unless it was necessary to save the life or health of the mother.

Chapter Three

Arguments against Legally Requiring a Pregnant Woman to Act in the Interests of her Future Child

The previous chapter argued that there are good reasons for claiming that a pregnant woman has both moral and legal duties to act in the interests of her future child, and it argued further that these obligations fall into two stages: During the first stage, she would be expected to assume only minimal burdens, while during the second stage the burdens may be greater. To understand and assess this proposed hierarchy of obligations more fully, we need to contrast a woman's obligations at three different phases: 1) when she is not pregnant, 2) when she is pregnant but it is not clear that she will carry the pregnancy to term (and she may legally obtain an abortion for any reason), and 3) when it is clear that she will carry the pregnancy to term (i.e., the pregnancy is so advanced that she may legally get an abortion only to save her own life and/or health). The first part of this chapter examines issues peculiar to phases one and two; the second and longer part analyzes more general arguments against permitting state intervention into the lives of pregnant women that take all three phases into account.

Arguments against Permitting State Interference with a Pregnant Woman During the First Stage of Pregnancy

Let us begin with two simple but troublesome truths. The first is a matter of logic: To hold women to different standards of behavior depending on whether or not they are pregnant requires that the women *know* that they are pregnant. The second is a matter of fact: Many women are pregnant for months before they are aware of their condition (this is true for drug addicts, for instance, a large percentage of whom have irregular menstrual cycles and/or pay little attention to the timing of their menses) [39]. Thus, if we want pregnant women to act in the interests of their future children even during the first few months of gestation, we confront a set of unappealing choices: 1) We require a woman to fulfill an obligation (e.g., reduce alcohol and tobacco intake) she does not know she has (because she does not know she is pregnant); or, 2) we require all women (pregnant or not) to uphold standards that are applied to *no* men (that is, we require all women to act as though they were pregnant, in order to ensure compliance during the early months of pregnancy); or, 3) we require only those pregnant women who are conscientious enough to seek medical care – and who thus have provided proof of their pregnancies – to abide by these standards, and permit other pregnant women to act however they wish. (Before her condition is apparent to anyone else, a woman who knows she is pregnant yet does not wish to adapt her lifestyle for the sake of her future child could always deny that she was aware of her condition). Our choices, then, are as follows: Either we 1) demand the impossible, 2) discriminate against all women, or 3) provide a strong incentive for women to avoid seeking prenatal care.

In addition, a woman's legal right to seek an abortion at this stage creates a variety of dilemmas. The previous chapter argued that, although a pregnant woman may not have *carte blanche* to behave however she wishes, she may circumvent the imposition of unwanted medical treatments or lifestyle changes by having an abortion (at least during the early stage of pregnancy). This position carries two disquieting ramifications.

First, some women would choose to have abortions simply in order to avoid having to accede to someone else's notion of reasonable due care, and hence the number of abortions may increase. It is not unlikely that a woman in the grip of an addiction, for instance, would choose to have an abortion rather than enter a treatment program. Anyone who is against abortion in principle would find this prospect alarming; indeed, advocates of a fetus's 'right to life' may want to prohibit coercive measures aimed at preventing prenatal harms for fear that more women would choose to have abortions rather than alter their behavior. In addition, it is one thing for the state to allow abortions; it is quite another for the state to adopt policies which are likely to prompt additional abortions.

The other troubling feature of the argument so far is based on exactly the opposite concern: Although women have the legal right to seek an abortion, many are unable to exercise that right. Part of the problem is that abortions cost money, and not all women who wish to have an abortion can afford the procedure. Although some state Medicaid programs pay for abortions, many of them do not, and the U.S. Supreme Court has upheld this denial of benefits.[1] In addition, even before the Supreme Court's decision in *Webster*, and certainly since, physicians have been reluctant to perform abortions after about twenty weeks gestation (even though no fetus is viable at that point). So those women who fail to realize in time that they are pregnant, and those who realize it but cannot decide how to deal with it in time, may be unable to find a physician willing to perform the procedure. The harsh reality, then, is that many women who desperately want an abortion do not have access to the procedure. Were society to impose upon pregnant women the legal obligation to conform to a standard of due care during all stages of pregnancy, a good number of women would find themselves obligated to accept further burdens on pregnancies they already regard as oppressive but which they are unable to terminate.

These are realistic concerns, and they provide additional reasons for keeping the legal requirements of due care at a minimum and imposing no significant burdens. Indeed, I would argue that the combination of all of these factors outweighs the arguments in favor of recognizing a legal duty on a pregnant women's part to act in the interests of her child-to-be at this early stage of pregnancy (although her moral duty remains).

General Arguments against Permitting State Intervention into the Lives of Pregnant Women

Three recent California cases are illustrative of the concerns of both those who are in favor of and those who oppose state intervention to prevent prenatal harms. In the first two cases, criminal charges were brought against women because they caused prenatal harms to their children; in the third case, the state actively intervened to extend physical confinement of a pregnant woman in order to prevent prenatal harm.

Heroin Addiction

Margaret Reyes was a heroin addict and pregnant with twins when, near term, she was told by a public health nurse that her continued use of heroin and refusal to seek prenatal care would jeopardize the health and perhaps even the life of her children. Ms. Reyes ignored the warning, and her children were born addicted to heroin and suffering from withdrawal symptoms. Ms. Reyes was arrested and charged with felony child endangerment under Section 273a of the California Penal Code. This statute reads, in part,

> Any person who, under circumstances or conditions likely to produce great bodily harm or death,...having the care or custody of any child,...willfully causes or permits such child to be placed in such situation that its person or health is endangered, is punishable by imprisonment.

There are two ways the statute could have been applied in this case. The first would be to extend it to include the protection of fetuses. That is, one could interpret the reference to 'any child' in the statute as pertaining to the unborn as well as the born. The court, however, firmly rejected this interpretation: The statute includes no mention of a fetus, the court pointed out, and if state legislators had intended this statute to apply to fetuses, they would have said so explicitly. Indeed, the court noted that the fetus is not included in any of California's criminal statutes:

> [A]n unborn child has been held not to be a 'human being' within contemplation of the murder statute...or the manslaughter statute...an unborn child has been said not to be included in the designation 'minor child' in the failure to provide statute...an unborn child has been held not to be a 'person' as that word is used in the Fourteenth Amendment to the United States Constitution...the United States Supreme Court has held an unborn child is not a 'dependent child' within the meaning of the Aid to Families with Dependent Children provisions [291].

Hence the court rejected the contention that the felony child endangerment statute applied to fetuses. Although the court invited lawmakers to amend the statute to include fetuses, state legislators have not done so.

The prosecution also presented an alternative interpretation of the case: This was not a case of harm to two fetuses, but rather the case concerned harm to living children. Although the harmful *acts* were committed before the children were born, the prosecution argued, the *effects* of the acts were not realized until after birth, when the children were separate from their mother and recognized as persons under the law. But the court rejected this interpretation as well, basing its conclusion on the fact that Ms. Reyes did nothing to harm her children after they were born, when the law recognizes them as persons worthy of protection:

> It is not contended that petitioner did anything to endanger the persons or health of the children after their birth, and if petitioner placed the children in such a situation that their persons or health were endangered, she did so when she used heroin and failed to seek prenatal medical care during the last two months of her pregnancy, that is, when the children were yet unborn [291, p. 913].

The court concluded therefore that Ms. Reyes's actions while she was pregnant were not proscribed by the child endangerment statute.

This second move by the court is interesting in the light of the treatment of prenatal harms in tort law. Recall that, as explained in Chapter One, every state recognizes a prenatal negligent act or omission which shows up as injury later as a legitimate cause for bringing forward a civil suit. That is, all states recognize claims made for compensation on behalf of children who incurred injuries prenatally and were born alive. Had this been a civil suit, then, the outcome of the case might have been quite different, for there was no disagreement as to the deleterious effects of Ms. Reyes's actions on her children. However, because this was a criminal case, not a civil one, the court was limited to appealing to relevant state criminal statutes, since fetal endangerment is not a common law crime.

It is not surprising that the court rejected the prosecution's interpretation of this case, since criminal statutes are ordinarily applied strictly in order to respond to the requirements of due process. The question now is: Should the criminal law reflect the same concerns as the tort law? In other words, given that Ms. Reyes's drug use (which harmed her children) would be recognized as actionable in a civil court, should it be made a criminal offense?

Negligence

In November 1985, when Pamela Rae Stewart was approximately 33 weeks pregnant, she sought medical care for vaginal bleeding. Her physician diagnosed a condition of placenta previa, and prescribed a standard course of treatment: She should stay off her feet as much as possible, refrain from sexual intercourse, take regular doses of a certain medication designed to suppress early labor, and seek medical care immediately if she begins to bleed again.

Less than two weeks later, Ms. Stewart gave birth to a severely brain-damaged child, who survived for only about five weeks. In September

1986 – almost ten months after the infant's death – Ms. Stewart was arrested and charged with fetal abuse.

Exactly what happened prior to the child's birth is a matter of dispute. The prosecution claimed that Ms. Stewart had not taken her medication as instructed, that she had intercourse with her husband against doctor's orders, that the bleeding was a result of having had intercourse, and that she had been bleeding for twelve hours before she reached the hospital. In addition, the prosecution contended, amphetamines were found in the infant's system. The prosecution concluded that these actions caused the death of the child, and decided to bring criminal charges against Ms. Stewart.

Rather than using the child endangerment statute, however, since it had been rejected by the court in the *Reyes* case, the prosecution this time used a different part of the California penal code, Section 270, which reads in part:

> Every parent of any child who willfully omits, without lawful excuse, to perform any duty imposed upon him by law, to furnish necessary food, clothing, shelter, or medical attendance for such child, is guilty of a misdemeanor....A child conceived but not yet born is an existing person so far as this section is concerned.

Ms. Stewart's description of what happened differed considerably from that of the prosecution. Although Ms. Stewart admitted that she had had sexual relations with her husband, and that she had begun to bleed soon afterward, she contended that she had rushed immediately to the hospital. She also claimed that she had continued to take the prescribed medication, and that the drugs in the child's system were antihistamines, not amphetamines. Her main defense, however, was not based on the facts of the case, but on the argument that Penal Code Section 270 was not applicable to her situation.

One of the defense's arguments was that employing Penal Code Section 270 in this manner fatally conflicted with legislative intent. The purpose of this section of the penal code was to enforce financial obligations, the defense claimed, not to ensure proper medical care or to punish neglectful parents. In addition, the defense argued, since this statute had never before been employed in the manner in which the prosecution now wished to use it, the defendant could not have known that it would be applied to her actions. Ms. Stewart had no warning – nor did anyone else – that the California penal code would be applied to prenatal harms. Thus, the defense concluded, the prosecution was guilty of applying *ex post facto* laws, and of violating the defendant's right to due process.

The court agreed with the defense, and ruled that Section 270 'does not impose the duty upon pregnant women to seek prenatal care' [113]. The ruling seems based on an appropriate interpretation of this particular statute: The California Supreme Court had ruled earlier that the primary purpose of the statute was to obtain financial support for children, and the statute had been used solely for that purpose since its enactment in 1872.

Our concern, however, is not only with the proper application of a particular statute in a particular case, but also with the more general issue of whether or not prenatal harms are appropriately and justifiably included in the range of criminal statutes and, if so, how such criminal treatment could best be structured to meet fairness standards and also fulfill the purposes of the criminal law. As the judge in the *Stewart* case noted, 'It would appear to the court that since the state has an interest in the health of an unborn child [in] the third trimester, the state Legislature could pass a statute protecting the health of an unborn child under narrow conditions' [113]. Many bills to that effect have been proposed in California, but none have passed into law.

Inability to Provide Basic Care

Kay Smith was homeless, mentally impaired, and pregnant. She previously had given birth to two children, both of whom had been taken by the state on the ground that she was unable to care for them. She now was institutionalized – she had been certified to be institutionalized for fourteen days – but was due to be released. When the Department of Public Social Services (DPSS) learned that Ms. Smith was going to be released before the birth of her child, it sought a court order to detain her in secure custody. DPSS argued that both Ms. Smith and her future child would be at jeopardy were she released before the birth of the child.

The case was heard in juvenile court on May 6, 1980, the day Ms. Smith was due to be released from the mental institution. The court found that the fetus was a 'child' under the provisions of the state child welfare code, and ordered that the fetus be kept under detention until its birth; thus Ms. Smith, too, was ordered to be kept institutionalized. She was maintained in the mental ward of a hospital for over six weeks, until she delivered on June 23, 1980.

The case was appealed – and although the California State Court of Appeals dismissed the appeal as moot because Ms. Smith could not be found and because the child had been born – it did rule on the actions of the lower court. Among its most important findings, the Court of Appeals determined that a fetus is *not* a child within the meaning of the California child welfare statute, and so the order of the juvenile court had no statutory authority [271].

Discussion

Proponents of state intervention look to cases like these to support their arguments. In the Pamela Rae Stewart case, for example, her physician's list of instructions does not seem unduly burdensome: She was told to take a certain medication for a couple of weeks, refrain from having sexual intercourse, refrain from ingesting illegal drugs, and get as much rest as possible. Advocates of state intervention question which is likely to cause more harm: requiring her by law to follow these instructions or not requiring her to do so. We must weigh the relatively minor inconvenience and discomfort to Ms. Stewart, it is contended, against the death of a child who, had his mother behaved differently, would presumably be alive and healthy today. This is a utilitarian calculation: We weigh the possible harms and benefits, and choose the alternative that would produce the least harm and/or the greatest benefit.

A legitimate goal of state intervention with pregnant women is the prevention of harm to their future children. And the guiding concern behind the intervention is in principle the welfare of these children. But as we shall see from a closer examination of the above cases, efforts to act on these laudable intentions must be scrutinized carefully: State intervention may cause more harm than it prevents; it may discriminate unfairly against pregnant women; and a professed interest in the welfare of children may mask a more controversial attitude toward the place of women in society.

Of those who argue against state intervention to prevent prenatal harms, most hold that *no* interventions should be allowed. They would probably agree with Martha Field's contention that 'No maternal action, not even drug abuse, should justify pre- or post-birth sanctions for pregnant women's behavior' [86]. As with arguments in favor of state intervention to prevent prenatal harms, there are a variety of arguments available against state intervention. We shall analyze four of the strongest positions: 1) those which appeal to the rights of pregnant women, 2) those employing consequentialist calculations, 3) those based on a claim of unfair discrimination, and 4) those appealing to the problems of drafting and implementing fair, workable laws.

Rights of Pregnant Women

The Rights of Liberty and Privacy

Arguments against state interference with the lives of pregnant women in order to prevent prenatal harms are often couched in terms of the women's rights of liberty and/or privacy. Dawn E. Johnsen, for instance, avers that, 'The magnitude of the intrusion on women's rights threatened by the current expansion of fetal rights implicates basic constitutional liberty and privacy interests that have been recognized by the Court in *Roe* and in other cases' [118, p. 614]; while Lawrence J. Nelson and Nancy Milliken [168, p. 1065] state that, 'The philosophical question confronting society is whether it wishes to enforce a policy that would entail on an unprecedented scale serious invasions of a woman's privacy, restriction of her civil liberties, and interference with her religious and personal beliefs;' and Janet Gallagher [99, p. 107] points out that, 'Court intervention may mean drastic invasion, not only of women's bodies but of their liberty.'

Government invasion of individual liberty and privacy is nothing new, of course, and it occurs every minute of every day in America: We need a license from the state to drive our cars, a blood test before we can get married, a passport in order to travel abroad. Indeed, a large proportion of state rules infringe in some measure on the liberty and privacy of competent adults: We are not allowed to drive our vehicles faster than the posted speed limit, we are not allowed to walk naked down the corridors of high schools, we are not allowed to withhold intimate details of our financial interactions from the Internal Revenue Service, and our luggage and briefcases and purses are x-rayed by strangers every time we board a commercial aircraft. To claim, then, that state actions to prevent prenatal harms would infringe on the liberty and privacy of pregnant women is not to assert anything very alarming or even surprising.

But this is not the claim. The assertion is, rather, that the sort of state intervention we are considering would interfere *too much* with pregnant women's liberty and privacy, that it would infringe *unfairly* on these important rights. But what does this really mean? How, in other words, do we characterize the rights of liberty and privacy? And which infringements with them would be inappropriate and unfair?

Clearly the rights of liberty and privacy are not without limits. Nor are they distinctly and uncontroversially delineated. The term 'privacy,' for instance, does not appear anywhere in the U.S. Constitution or its Amendments. And Ronald Dworkin argues persuasively that it is 'absurd to suppose that men and women have any general right to liberty at all, at least as liberty has traditionally been conceived by its champions...as the absence of constraints placed by a government upon what a man might do if he wants to' [70, 71].

The scope and power of the 'rights' of liberty and privacy, in other words, are open to interpretation. One requirement of this interpretation is to distill which aspects of the terms are germane to the debate at hand. Without going into exegetical detail, I will simply assert that the notion of liberty relevant here is the freedom from unwanted touching (or the right to bodily integrity); and the relevant aspect of privacy involves private decision making (or the freedom from unwanted intrusion by the state into one's intimate affairs). These rights can be derived from the Fourth Amendment's prohibition against unreasonable searches and seizures, the Fourteenth Amendment's requirements of due process of law, the Ninth Amendment's recognition that the Constitution does not enumerate all rights 'retained by the people,' as well as from various aspects of the common law.

The right to bodily integrity is taken very seriously in our society, and as we shall see, it frequently is judged to outweigh important state interests. And the Supreme Court has recognized a right to private decision making in a number of cases, employing it as the foundation for ruling against a variety of laws: those forbidding parents to send their children to private schools [285], laws prohibiting married couples from using contraceptives [263], laws forbidding interracial marriages [278], and laws forbidding abortion [293].

The right of bodily integrity and the right of private decision making meet where medical treatments are involved, as evidenced by the widespread acceptance of the doctrine of informed consent within the medical community [78]. The use of this doctrine in the therapeutic setting gradually emerged from malpractice suits involving nonconsentual touching of a patient's body. In a famous 1914 case, for instance, the New

York Supreme Court ruled that, 'Every human being of adult years and sound mind has a right to determine what shall be done with his own body; and a surgeon who performs an operation without his patient's consent commits an assault, for which he is liable in damages' [295]. And in a more recent case, a Kansas court ruled that,

> Anglo-American law starts with the premise of thoroughgoing self-determination. It follows that each man is considered to be master of his own body, and he may, if he be of sound mind, expressly prohibit the performance of lifesaving surgery, or other medical treatment [282].

Indeed, courts have consistently ruled that physicians may not treat competent patients without their consent, irrespective of considerations of the quality of care. And in recent years all medical and research codes of ethics have held that physicians must obtain the informed consent of patients before undertaking invasive therapeutic or research procedures.

Although the presumption always should be in favor of respecting a person's right of bodily integrity and right of private decision making, it must be remembered that the courts have not regarded these as unqualified rights. Indeed, the U.S. Supreme Court has recognized as legitimate several instances of forced bodily intrusion without consent. The Court has upheld vaccinating and sterilizing people against their wills, for instance, as well as having blood samples taken [250, 251, 273, 296]. Lower courts have even allowed bullets to be removed from suspects in order to obtain evidence in criminal cases [249, 301, 302, 306]. This is not to say, of course, that the right of bodily integrity and the right of private decision making may easily be overridden, or even to suggest that all of these intrusions were justified; rather, the point is that, although these rights are very important indeed, they have not been recognized in the law as automatically outweighing all other considerations.

In making their determinations, courts generally weigh the individual's interests against the state's interests at stake in the particular case. Included also in the calculation are other relevant factors: whether there are less invasive alternatives to the proposed intrusion by which the state could achieve its goals, whether the intrusion will successfully yield the desired results, and whether the intrusion would have a major or minor impact on the individual.

Interestingly, courts generally have ruled that, even if there is no other way to meet the state's goal and the method proposed will be successful, bodily intrusions would not be permitted if they put the individual at substantial risk of harm. In allowing a blood sample to be taken from an individual, for instance, the Supreme Court noted that,

> The integrity of an individual's person is a cherished value of our society. That we today hold that the Constitution does not forbid the State's minor intrusions into an individual's body under stringently limited conditions in no way indicates that it permits more substantial intrusions, or intrusions under other conditions [296, p. 772].

In another case, the Court deemed the forced removal of a bullet from the left side of a felony suspect to be one of these unwarranted intrusions. The Court stated that a crucial factor in its determination was the severity of the proposed medical procedure, which would require the administration of a general anesthetic, and the extent to which the procedure might threaten the health of the individual [309]. And when asked to permit the forcible pumping of a criminal suspect's stomach, the Court responded in horror that the suggestion was 'conduct that shocks the conscience' [292].

The courts do not always look to the well-being of the individual, however. Some lower courts have ordered the administration of intrusive measures on one person for the sake of another, including requiring one individual to undergo medical treatment in order to benefit another. These range widely in degree of intrusion: from vaccinations to blood transfusions to cesarean sections to the removal of an internal organ [244, 274, 277, 289]. It would be instructive at this juncture to examine a case of a court-ordered removal of a body organ – a kidney – without the donor's consent.

Court-Ordered Removal of a Body Part

Twenty-eight year old Tommy Strunk needed a kidney transplant, and his physicians discovered that the most compatible donor was his brother Jerry, aged twenty-seven. Jerry, however, had an I.Q. of 35 (a mental age of about six) and was institutionalized. Their parents agreed that Jerry should donate one of his kidneys to his brother, but the case was taken to county court as a precautionary measure. In court, a consulting psychiatrist and a representative of the Department of Mental Health concurred with Mr. and Mrs. Strunk and so eventually did the judge. The court explained that Jerry was being ordered to donate a kidney because his 'well-being would be jeopardized more severely by the loss of his brother than by the removal of a kidney.' The circuit court – to which the case was appealed – concurred, and the operations were performed [303].

A careful reading of the court's opinion reveals that the best interests of the donor were not of primary concern. As one of the judges noted in his dissent,

> The majority opinion is predicated upon the finding of the circuit court that there will be psychological benefits to the ward but points out that the incompetent has the mentality of a six-year-old child. It is common knowledge beyond dispute that the loss of a close relative or a friend to a six-year-old child is not of major impact [303, p. 150].

Although the judge's psychological generalization may not be accurate, it does point out that there is a very strong burden of proof to be borne by those who say that the loss of a brother would cause more harm than the risks and pains of major surgery (especially to someone who cannot understand what is happening to him) and the permanent loss of a kidney. And it suggests that the risks to the donor were not given much weight. The court found the risks to Jerry's life of living with only one kidney to be equal to commuting sixteen miles a day by car. But the court did not seem to take seriously the other costs involved: the risks associated with undergoing major surgery and general anesthesia, the pain involved in recovery. There was another serious risk to Jerry as well: If he somehow lost normal functioning of his remaining kidney, dialysis would not have been available to him, for mentally retarded people in Kentucky were not offered dialysis treatment when this case occurred [57].[2]

The reason the court gave for permitting the organ transfer from Jerry to Tommy is also notable. The court argued that it was employing the doctrine of substituted judgment: that it was acting as Jerry Strunk would have acted were he competent to choose. As John Robertson explains,

> For over 150 years, the substituted judgment doctrine has regulated the judicial response to claims of needy relatives upon incompetents, and has permitted depletion of incompetent estates with no direct benefit to them solely to help others. The rationale for this practice – that respect for persons requires courts to follow the putative wishes of the incompetent were he otherwise, even if such a course provides no direct benefit to the incompetent – is *prima facie* relevant in determining whether tissue and organs may be taken from incompetents to benefit

> close relatives in need. If property can be invaded because of minimal risk to the incompetent's interest, then presumably the body could also be invaded if the risks are commensurate [189].

But this presumption is unsound. There is no justification for lumping property and body together, and there is no justification for maintaining that if it is legitimate to invade someone's property, it also is legitimate to invade his body.

So another way of understanding this case is that Jerry Strunk was simply used for the sake of his brother. This may have been true in another case as well, in which the court allowed a fourteen-year-old girl with Down's Syndrome to donate a kidney to her brother [277]. While these cases provide legal precedents for compelling one family member to undergo extremely invasive medical procedures for the sake of another family member, we should be very cautious about applying them to the question of whether pregnant women should be compelled to undergo treatment for the sake of their future children. In one very significant sense, the kidney donor cases and the forced treatment of pregnant women cases are incommensurate: The donors in the kidney cases were incompetent to decide for themselves, while in the typical case with which we are concerned, the pregnant women are competent to make their own decisions – and this competence stands as a strong reason against asking for the court's intervention (just as incompetence may be a good reason to seek a court ruling).

But this is not the only basis for caution in using the *Strunk* and *Little* cases to justify compelling a pregnant woman to undergo treatment for the sake of her future child. The kidney donor cases raise the very real concern that individuals, including pregnant women, may be used as mere means in order to benefit others. While using one person to benefit another is not always objectionable – most of us are regularly used as means to benefit others insofar as we are taxed to pay for social service programs from which we receive no direct assistance[3] – the cases at issue here involve considerably greater intrusion: intrusion into the very bodies of the individuals, not merely their wallets. Many people find this prospect offensive, especially in a country founded on the right of each individual to 'life, liberty, and the pursuit of happiness.' As one commentator asks, 'Could anything be as morally repugnant as physically restraining and tying down a pregnant woman who refused surgery?' [93].

The case of Robert McFall and David Shimp illustrates this stance (in contrast to the kidney donor cases). In 1978, thirty-nine-year old Robert McFall was diagnosed as having aplastic anemia, a condition which usually is fatal [19]. McFall's physician predicted that with a bone marrow transplant, McFall's chances of surviving a year would increase from 25 percent to between 40 and 60 percent. The doctor searched for a genetically compatible donor, and eventually came close to finding one in McFall's cousin, David Shimp. Shimp underwent the first series of tests, in which he was found to have tissue compatibility with McFall; but then Shimp refused to be tested further for genetic compatibility. So McFall sued Shimp, to try to compel him to donate some of his bone marrow. The court ruled against McFall, stating that,

> For a society which respects the rights of *one* individual, to sink its teeth into the jugular vein or neck of one of its members and suck from it sustenance for *another* member, is revolting to our hard-wrought concepts of jurisprudence. Forceable extraction of living body tissue causes revulsion to the judicial mind [280, p. 92].

McFall died of intracranial bleeding two weeks later.

Discussion

This section began by asking which infringements with a pregnant woman's rights of liberty and privacy would be inappropriate and unfair, and reviewed a series of legal cases as a first step towards an answer; but there are many other considerations which also must be taken into account before a conclusion can be drawn. As Chapter Two demonstrated, for instance, there are good reasons to assert that a woman does not have *carte blanche* to do whatever she wants while pregnant and that she may have certain moral and legal obligations towards her future child – obligations which do not play a part in any of the legal cases described above. In other words, because the proper response to the issue at hand – overriding a pregnant woman's preferences in order to protect the interests of her future child – calls for a balancing of interests, consequences, rights, and obligations, it is premature to conclude that a pregnant woman's rights of bodily integrity and private decision making may never be overridden. Yet since these rights are of such fundamental importance to our society, it should be clear that they may be abridged only in order to uphold something else that is of even greater importance. Thus the question for us – whether the protection of the interests of her future child is ever reason enough to override her rights of self-determination and privacy – remains open (Chapter Four will address this debate further).

Consequentialist Arguments

It was argued earlier that the state has a legitimate interest in the prevention of prenatal harms, and that this interest may be important enough to outweigh the pregnant woman's right to be left alone. If this were so, it would be the case only when state intervention could be expected to be successful: that is, only when state intervention would indeed prevent harm to the future child. The previous chapter noted the potential benefits to children of attempts to prevent prenatal harms; but there is also a plethora of potential negative effects on them and on their mothers.

Critics of state intervention claim that, instead of reducing suffering, state intervention in these cases will only increase it. A pregnant woman who fears that her physician will report her to state authorities might be unwilling to divulge the details of her life, for instance, to avoid unwanted limitations on her choices. She may even refrain from seeking medical care altogether. Many of these women have what are considered to be high-risk pregnancies, and they are precisely the women who need medical care the most.

It is conceivable, then, that coercive measures designed to help a child could result instead in discouraging his drug-abusing mother from obtaining prenatal care, or encouraging her to refrain from telling the truth about her condition to the physician. Other negative possibilities abound: 'Coercive measures may lead to concealed pregnancies, nonassisted births, an upsurge in abandonment, and even infanticide' [99, p. 214]. Were this the case, the big losers would be the children. In response to these and other 'potentially regrettable consequences of forced medical or surgical procedures,' the Committee on Bioethics of the American Academy of Pediatrics recommends that court intervention should be sought only 'in rare cases' and 'should be seen as a last resort to be undertaken with great caution' [7].

Although opponents of state interference take the possibility of these negative consequences as conclusive, it is important to note that instituting state involvement in prenatal matters may not have these effects. All fifty states require by law that many professionals – pediatricians, emergency room physicians, teachers, social workers – report suspected cases of child abuse to state authorities and thus initiate mechanisms designed to remove children from the custody of their parents, yet the efficacy of these professionals has not been destroyed. However, because there is a real possibility that something could go drastically wrong were pregnant women required by law to behave in certain ways, careful exploration of the social consequences is warranted before action is taken on a public policy level.

Methods of dealing with prenatal damage after it has occurred may also cause more harm than good. Bringing criminal charges against a woman for fetal abuse, for instance, may not have much deterrent effect, for the choices of many pregnant women – such as the three described at the beginning of this chapter – are often not amenable to rational incentives. And criminal sanctions may be counterproductive: The newborn of a woman in jail would be without his mother during crucial bonding stages, and a mother who is imprisoned after the birth of her son because of harm she caused him while pregnant may thereby resent him and may mistreat him should she regain custody.[4]

It is also important to note that other methods exist for reducing the incidence of prenatal harm, methods which are likely to be more successful than the coercive measures discussed above. Many prenatal harms are not caused intentionally, but instead are the result of the mother's ignorance about the special circumstances of pregnancy: the nutritional requirements, the effects of certain drugs, the consequences of maternal infections, and so on. Health education, then, is an important element in the prevention of prenatal harms. It should be required of all school children, and made available to everyone else (and for girls, at least, the classes should emphasize the special needs of pregnant women).

Education will not solve the problem of preventable prenatal harms, of course, for some pregnant women will continue to pay insufficient attention to the welfare of the children they will bear even though they are aware of the consequences of their acts. One likely explanation for this behavior is that the women do not wish to be pregnant. And the proper response to this is obvious: Improve methods of contraception, make them more easily affordable and more widely available, and reduce the barriers to abortion during the first trimester of pregnancy. A consequentialist calculation of the net benefits of these measures in relation to more coercive measures (such as threatening to imprison a mother after the birth of an impaired child) would no doubt rank the former as preferable: They will reduce the incidence of prenatal harm with few negative repercussions.

The 'Slippery Slope' Arguments

A different sort of consequentialist argument is called the 'slippery slope' argument. There are two parts to this argument, what we may call the *logical* version and the *practical* version.

The logical version of the slippery slope argument says, in effect, that it is not possible to formulate a principle which will permit just the actions we want to permit while also excluding all those we want to exclude. Thus, unless we wish to allow the state to interfere in every aspect of a pregnant woman's life, we must not take the first step – we must not permit any intrusion at all into a pregnant woman's liberty – for that would also logically commit us to permitting the most severe and most unjust interferences with her liberty as well.

The strength of this argument lies in the accuracy of the statement that there are no good reasons for accepting some intrusions with a pregnant woman's liberty while rejecting others. But is this true? Are there really no rational grounds for distinguishing one type of state interference from another in these cases? The answer lies in an examination of a set of related factors which must be considered before the conclusion can be drawn that any intervention is truly justified. These include the requirements of due process of law and proportionality (which weighs the nature and extent of the harm to be prevented, the probability that it will occur, the probability that it can be avoided, and the degree of the intrusion). Limits have been set in other types of cases: The Supreme Court makes a distinction, for instance, between the minor invasion of taking a blood sample from a suspect and the major invasion of pumping his stomach, and legislators of every state in the nation believe that a line can be drawn between the legitimate exercise of parental discretion and the illegitimate infliction of child abuse. The previous chapter argued that rational limits can be set in pregnancy cases as well, but no doubt these limits would not satisfy those who oppose all state interventions into the activities of pregnant women.

The other version of the slippery slope argument – which is characterized as the 'practical' version – is based on predictions of outcomes, not logic. The basic contention of this argument is that, once we allow any intrusion at all into the lives of pregnant women, even intrusions of the most minor sort, then other, more morally questionable intrusions will in fact follow: We will continue to change and loosen our principles as we become psychologically accustomed to what previously seemed extraordinary and unacceptable. First a pregnant woman might be forbidden to take certain illegal drugs known to cause fetal damage, then she might be forbidden to use other, otherwise legal, teratogenic substances such as alcohol and tobacco. Then the state might require her to take certain vitamins and eat certain foods: The importance of maternal nutrition during pregnancy has been well-documented [54, 56, 163, 178, 196]. Eventually the state would prohibit her from taking some over-the-counter drugs (such as cough medicines and aspirin), require her to get a certain number of hours of bedrest, monitor her sexual activity, and so on. Indeed, the argument goes, potentially almost everything a pregnant woman does will be open to state control (since almost everything a pregnant woman does may cause prenatal harm).

How could conformity to these strictures be ensured? George Annas suggests that, 'Effectively monitoring compliance would require confining pregnant women to an environment in which eating, exercise, drug use, and sexual intercourse could be controlled. This could, of course, be a maximum security country club' [11]. After all, could we trust a pregnant woman who is addicted to nicotine to cease smoking simply because a judge ordered her to do so? And would not a drug addict be more likely to hide than to submit to weekly urine tests? The only way we can be certain that pregnant women are not doing anything that will harm their future children is to monitor their every activity.

But, as Annas points out, 'such massive invasions of privacy can only be justified by treating pregnant women during their pregnancy as nonpersons' [11]. This is not paranoia speaking. The history of women is fraught with domination and subjugation and denial of basic rights: In the past, women in this country could not hold public office, serve on juries, or bring suit in their own names; women could not practice law, or bartend, or work extended hours; women could not even vote. All of these restrictions have since been lifted in the United States, but the worry remains that the attitude behind them – which views men and women as fundamentally dissimilar, with distinct social roles to play – still persists.

The view that men and women are intrinsically different is an old and familiar one. And the implications drawn from it – that men belong in the public world of work while women belong in the home caring for their families – is one many people find appealing. But while this view of the distinctive spheres of men and women reflects a very common world view, it is not a world view that is universally accepted or appreciated. And it is certainly not a world view that should be imposed on those who do not share it, at least in our pluralistic society, where many people believe that, with regard to social roles, there are no significant differences between men and women. It would be unfair, then, to impose one set of values on people who do not share them, to treat all women as though their primary function were to propagate the species and thereby to deny them access to alternative life styles.

The Claim of Unfair Discrimination

This brings us to a related concern: that laws requiring pregnant women to behave in certain ways are unfairly discriminatory. The protest here is that requiring a pregnant woman to act on behalf of her future child imposes restraints on her freedom that are materially different from other socially accepted limitations on people's activities, and even materially different from other accepted limitations on her own activities when she is not pregnant.

One basic contention is that it is unjust to demand things of pregnant women that are demanded of no one else in society. No man, for instance, is required to undergo any kind of bodily invasion at all for the sake of someone else. The advent of organ and tissue transplantation techniques highlights this situation: No competent adult is legally required to give a kidney or bone marrow or blood to any other person, be it stranger or close family member, even if denial of help means the death of that individual [187].[5]

A person may even refuse to donate a life-saving organ after death. Dead bodies are not considered legitimate sources of transplantable organs if the deceased had refused while alive to be a donor or if the family of the deceased declines to allow the organs to be removed. Although we may question the validity of this stance, it is unlikely that this rule will be altered in the near future. In a recent survey, over 86 percent of those polled declared that physicians should not have the power to remove organs from those deceased who had not signed organ donor cards, without consulting the next of kin [77, p. ES-33]. Many people see this power as too coercive. Their argument – and it is one that has found strong political support – is that our society places such an emphasis on individual liberty that people should be free to refuse to donate their organs after death and free to refuse to donate the organs of a deceased relative.

One result of this policy is a severe shortage of transplantable organs in this country. It has been estimated that at any one time, between 8,000 and 10,000 people are waiting for a donor organ to become available [227]. A large proportion of these people will never receive the organs upon which their lives depend. If cadavers are not routinely used to benefit others, and people die as a result, then pregnant women should not be used to benefit others either. Indeed, there is 'no good reason why pregnant women should be treated with less respect than corpses' [168, p. 1065].

The argument grounded on the claim of unfair discrimination, then, is straightforward: If no individual, alive or dead, need undergo any sort of bodily intrusion against his or her will for the sake of another person, including a relative, then it is unjust to insist that a pregnant woman undertake a comparable form of medical treatment against her will for the sake of another person, including a future person.[6]

Difficulty of Drafting and Implementing Legislation

Legitimate state intervention into the lives of pregnant women presupposes that the women have been put on notice that society expects them to meet a reasonable standard of due care and will not tolerate certain activities. One effective way to do this is through legislation: Certain behaviors of pregnant women could be legally proscribed through a body of 'crimes against the fetus' statutes [51, 177]. Indeed, such laws are necessary if criminal penalties are to be imposed, since crimes in this country are set by statute, not through the common law (as are torts).

Statutorily prohibiting prenatal harms in general would not work, in part because some prenatal harms simply cannot be avoided: There are certain deleterious conditions for which no medical treatment exists, for instance, or that cannot be detected in time to permit intervention.[7] The law, then, should speak only to that set of prenatal harms that can be prevented. Ideally, the law would include all and only those whose behavior we wish to change and exclude those whom we believe it is improper to coerce.

As a point of departure, consider the actions of Pamela Rae Stewart, as described by the prosecutor:

> Defendant's concealed argument is that a mother, with impunity, may ignore the warnings of her doctor despite the knowledge that she is experiencing a problem pregnancy. She may ply her body with dangerous, illegal and harmful drugs with no thought to its effect on the helpless human being growing in her womb. She may subject herself to the rigors of sexual intercourse without concern for the effect on the baby. And even though specifically warned, she may lay bleeding for hours without seeking available medical attention as her baby is deprived of its only source of nourishment. Such extreme disregard for any other human life, not to mention one whose only chance of survival depends upon the mother who carries him, approaches the level of maliciousness and conscious disregard for human life, which would properly support a second-degree murder conviction, not to mention one for a violation of Penal Code section 270 [284].

Let us assume for the sake of argument that the prosecutor has accurately described the facts. What precisely did Ms. Stewart do that was so terribly wrong? She stopped taking her prescribed medication, she had intercourse with her husband, she took some sort of drug (the prosecutor claims amphetamines, Ms. Stewart claims antihistamines), and she postponed seeking medical care. Except for taking amphetamines (which she denies), Ms. Stewart's actions were not especially troublesome, yet the combination of factors resulted in the birth of a severely brain-damaged child who died in infancy.

Could we devise a law (or set of laws) that would speak to analogous cases yet exclude women who have good reasons to engage in similar activities? Surely we do not want to prohibit by statute sexual relations between consenting adults (especially married couples); nor can we reasonably put limits on how much time may lapse between the realization that medical care may be needed and the seeking of such care: There are, after all, a large number of quite acceptable reasons for postponing medical care, one of which is the sensible judgment that whatever is wrong is not wrong enough to warrant the bother and expense of professional treatment.

So the proposal for dealing with cases such as Ms. Stewart's through a set of laws dealing with particular activities – sexual relations between consenting adults, judgments about the need for medical care, and so on – is untenable. Such laws would intrude too much on the privacy and autonomy of all of us. Instead, it might make sense to address these cases in light of her one over-arching failure: She failed to follow her physician's instructions. The proposal, then, is to require pregnant women to conform to their physicians' recommendations.

But would we really want to make criminal all failures to follow a physician's advice? After all, physicians are not invariably correct. In the past, they routinely prescribed x-rays and diuretics for pregnant women, for instance, practices that are discouraged today. And medical interventions accepted today are fraught with uncertainties as well, as the American College of Obstetricians and Gynecologists points out:

> Medical knowledge and judgment have limitations and fallibility, which the obstetrician must recognize when assigning clinical risks and benefits in order to advise patients. Methods for detecting fetal distress or deterioration are not always reliable indicators of poor outcome; therefore, assigning a degree of risk to the fetus is difficult. In addition, expected benefits for the fetus cannot always be achieved [53].

The prevalence of uncertainties in medicine stands as a strong disincentive for requiring by law that a pregnant woman follow her physician's advice.

Perhaps, though, it should be illegal for a pregnant woman to ignore a physician's recommendation when doing so causes prenatal harm. The woman, in other words, could be punished after the fact. But even when a physician's diagnosis is accurate and his or her recommended treatment course is the standard one, a policy of punishing a woman for having failed to conform has serious problems. The first is that, unless medical care is provided free-of-charge, we must expect that there will be legitimate financial reasons for not following some physicians' instructions. We could hardly fault a pregnant woman for not purchasing a prescription drug she believed she could not afford, or for not quitting the job she needs to support her family in order to obtain the recommended number of hours of bedrest. In addition, if we permit physicians to make decisions for pregnant women, we give them unprecedented power over one group of people, power that they do not have over any other. Physicians have the legal and moral duty to obtain the informed consent of all competent patients, including pregnant women. To make an exception to the informed consent rule in the case of pregnant women would be to discriminate unfairly against them.

The type of law we have been considering is too dangerously vague to be taken seriously. It would also probably be unconstitutional. As the

Supreme Court has noted, 'A vague law impermissibly delegates basic policy matters to policemen, judges and juries for resolution on an *ad hoc* and subjective basis with discriminatory application' [262, p. 109]. The worry that such laws would be open to discriminatory implementation and abuse is not an idle one. The case of Kay Smith, described at the beginning of this chapter, is instructive. First, her rights of due process were violated when her case was heard in a juvenile court – which is not constituted to handle cases of the mental competence of adults – and so she was not judged according to the specific statutes which determine the state's right to restrict her liberty due to her mental illness. Second, although lawyers for the state argued in court that Ms. Smith's pregnancy was very near term and that her detention would therefore last approximately only a fortnight, she in fact remained institutionalized for more than six weeks. One has to wonder if the stage of her pregnancy was misrepresented so that the state's proposal would appear less onerous to her.[8]

And it is probably not a coincidence that all three of the cases described at the beginning of this chapter involved women who were poor: Almost all of the pregnant women who have been subject to state intervention have been indigent or disadvantaged in some way. A national study conducted in 1987 showed that, of the twenty-one cases in which court orders were sought to intervene in the decisions of pregnant women, all of them involved women who were receiving public assistance or who were treated in a teaching-hospital clinic. In addition, 81 percent of the women were minorities (African, Asian or Hispanic), and 24 percent spoke English as a second language [125].

Another study – this one conducted on women who enrolled for prenatal care in one Florida county in 1989 – raises the question of discriminatory implementation of the law even more pointedly [40]. The researchers concluded that, although white women are just as likely to use drugs and alcohol during pregnancy as black women, blacks are much more likely to be reported to state authorities for drug use than whites:

> The proportion of white women reported for any drug use (48 of 4290 who delivered live-born infants) was 1.1 percent, whereas the proportion of black women reported for any drug use (85 of 793) was 10.7 percent. Thus, a black woman was 9.6 times more likely than a white woman to be reported for substance abuse during pregnancy. The difference was evident despite the fact that in the population we surveyed the frequency of positive results on toxicologic testing of urine samples obtained at the first prenatal visit was similar for white women (15.4 percent) and black women (14.1 percent) [40, p. 1204].

The authors of the study were unable to explain their results – but unfair discrimination would not be a bad guess.

One alternative to instituting vague laws that are open to discriminatory implementation and abuse is to spell out precisely what activities are prohibited and/or required. To accomplish this, however, we must abandon the goal of developing laws which would include a wide variety of prenatal harms – since, as pointed out above, the state's power to interfere with individuals' lives would be too great – and instead adopt the less onerous task of developing laws that cover a few specific prenatal harms. The case of Margaret Reyes is relevant here. Ms. Reyes ingested heroin during her pregnancy, and her twin children were born with heroin addictions. Since heroin is already considered to be an illegal substance, and since ingesting an illegal substance while pregnant is a straightforward action easy to describe, designing a statute prohibiting it seems relatively unproblematic.

The trouble with this proposal, however, is that we again run the risk of being arbitrary: Only those activities which we are able to describe satisfactorily in a statute will be prohibited or required, while equally harmful behavior goes unchallenged simply because it cannot be codified adequately.

Finally, before we decide to invoke the criminal law as a social response to prenatal harms – before we decide to create a new class of criminal – we should be certain that there is a strong preponderance of reasons in favor of doing so, for to be given a criminal status in our society is to be given a condemnation; indeed, we often refer to it as being 'branded' a criminal. Joel Feinberg calls this the 'expressive function [of punishment]: punishment is a conventional device for the expression of attitudes of resentment and indignation, and of judgments of disapproval and reprobation' [80, p. 98]. This chapter has argued that there is no such preponderance of reasons in favor of criminal legislation; indeed, this chapter has argued that the balance falls against regarding pregnant women as potential criminals. But even if the arguments fail to persuade that the balance of reasons lies against criminalizing certain activities of pregnant women, at least it should go far in showing that a clear preponderance of reasons in support of criminal legislation does not exist.

Conclusion

This chapter has argued that there are compelling reasons against allowing the state to intervene with the activities of pregnant women even when it is clear that their children will be carried to term: The state should not monitor a pregnant woman's activities in order to prevent harm to or promote the well-being of her future child, nor should it criminalize certain activities of pregnant women because they cause prenatal harms. These conclusions are based on a variety of arguments: 1) a woman's fundamental rights of bodily integrity and private decision making should not be subordinated to the welfare of someone else; 2) requiring pregnant women to behave in certain ways will have seriously negative consequences: pregnant women will be unwilling to be candid with their physicians, or they will not seek prenatal care at all, the number of abortions will increase, or grave hardships will be imposed on already burdened pregnant women; 3) a few reasonable limitations on the activities of pregnant women will lead inevitably to many unjust and onerous limitations (the 'slippery slope' arguments); 4) it is not fair to demand things of pregnant women that are demanded of no one else in society, so requiring pregnant women to behave in certain ways or risk legal penalties is unfairly discriminatory; and 5) the obstacles to drafting and implementing fair, workable laws seem insurmountable.

Of course, not all of the arguments presented here are compelling. One could argue, for instance, that it is not impossible to draft responsible laws which would make at least some of a pregnant woman's obligations to her future child clear and not unduly burdensome: After all, other laws considered by many people to be necessary – including child abuse and neglect laws – require equal subtlety and raise similar concerns. And the fact that all prenatal harms cannot be prevented is not reason enough to forgo preventing any of them.

In addition, we should be cautious about concluding that laws limiting the liberty of pregnant women are bound to be abused: It is not clear that imposing some minimal legal requirements of due care on pregnant women would inevitably lead to the imposition of unfair burdens. Chapter Two argued for the opposite position, that a legal duty of due care on the part of a pregnant woman with regard to the child she will bear should be recognized and that this duty – which is based on a standard of reasonableness – would not be unduly onerous. Indeed, while 'slippery slope' arguments should be taken seriously, since the potential for abuse in these cases is real, they should not be taken too seriously: It is possible to conjure up potentially terrible consequences for every public policy initiative, even the most benign.

So some of the arguments in this chapter are stronger and more reliable than others. An important question at this juncture is whether any combination of them is strong enough to justify the position that state interference into the activities of pregnant women is always wrong (because such interference would violate important rights of pregnant women), unfair (because the rules cannot be enforced impartially), or useless (because more harm than good would be produced in the process). If this is the case, then it would be consistent to advocate as a public policy position that state intervention into the lives of pregnant women in order to prevent prenatal harms should *never* be allowed. The arguments in this chapter, however, may not have shown that all types of state intervention to prevent prenatal harms are improper, but only that many of them are. Indeed, I believe that this chapter has presented a strong array of reasons to conclude that, even though a pregnant woman has moral obligations to act in the interests of her future child throughout her pregnancy, there are compelling reasons against legally requiring her to meet certain standards of due care before it is uncontroversially clear that she intends to bring the pregnancy to term. This conclusion has far-reaching implications for state intervention: The state would not be justified in acting to prevent some very serious prenatal harms during the early stage of a woman's pregnancy.

The issue now, then, is the strength of the arguments against state intervention during the later stage of pregnancy (the stage at which her moral duties are most strong because she clearly will be carrying the pregnancy to term). Perhaps some state interventions to prevent prenatal harms at this stage are warranted. It is the object of the following chapter to synthesize the arguments presented so far, and relate them to concrete cases.

Notes

[1] The U.S. Supreme Court has ruled that individual states may limit state Medicaid funding to medically necessary abortions [279] or to abortions necessary to save the mother's life [308]; states are not required to make public hospitals available for elective abortions and may bar public employees from participating in elective abortions [307]; and Congress may ban the use of federal Medicaid funds for abortions except when necessary to save the mother's life [264].

[2] Dialysis machines – artificial kidneys – were very strictly rationed in the days before Medicare assumed responsibility for the cost of that treatment.
[3] A libertarian – who believes the role of the state is to protect our negative rights, not to confer positive benefits on individuals – would of course argue that taxes to provide social benefits are indeed objectionable. Obviously, that is not the view I espouse. See Chapter Four, Note 33, for a brief discussion.
[4] Someone who believes that punishment is justified because the guilty deserve to be punished (who holds, in other words, a retributivist theory of punishment) would most likely be indifferent to these potential negative effects of punishing a mother for having caused prenatal harms, and would instead argue that, if she wrongfully caused harm, then she should be punished, regardless of the consequences. This is not the position presumed here.

There are two telling criticisms of this type of retributivist stance. One could argue that, even though the woman may deserve punishment, it does not follow that she should be punished, since countervailing considerations – such as the disbenefits to her child – may be more important. Thus one may reasonably conclude that it is better not to punish her at all, but to deal with the problem in some other way. Alternatively, one could claim that punishment is never morally good (since it is an infliction of harm), and it is justified only if its 'good' consequences (e.g., deterrence of undesirable activity) outweigh its 'bad' consequences (e.g., the punished women are harmed and their infants are left without their mothers). I am suggesting here that punishing women for having caused prenatal harm is likely to have more disbenefits than benefits.
[5] In the cases mentioned above, where a kidney was taken from one family member (without his consent) to give to another, the donors were incompetent to decide for themselves.
[6] Several types of bodily invasion – required by the state against the will of the individual – were mentioned above. The issue, though, is not what has been done, but what should be done. Chapter Four will explore the matter further.
[7] This raises the issue of the value of recognizing a right not to be born, mentioned briefly in Chapter Two, Note 7.
[8] I am not arguing that Ms. Smith should have been released before the birth of her child. A homeless, mentally impaired, near-term pregnant woman who cannot care for herself should be a legitimate exception to a rule forbidding state intervention. The point is, rather, that the procedure for deciding her fate was seriously flawed, and so her rights of due process were violated. Even though the presence of due process very likely would have produced the identical outcome in Ms. Smith's case, the state should have adhered to the requirements of due process, under the theory that following the correct procedure will produce the desired (i.e., fair) outcome considerably more often than will ignoring the requirements of due process.

Chapter Four

Practical Applications

In order to prevent serious prenatal harms, the state could employ any number of interventions into the lives of pregnant women. The previous chapters have explored many of these in an abstract way, concentrating on general moral and legal principles and public policy concerns. This chapter, however, will delve into the practical implications of the arguments presented so far, and will analyze some concrete cases. All of the options for interfering with a woman's liberty in order to prevent prenatal harms cannot be explored here – these are too numerous and diverse to permit comprehensive consideration – so a representative sampling has been chosen: requiring pregnant women to undergo cesarean sections, requiring pregnant drug abusers to enter residential treatment programs, preventing women from working with reproductive hazards in the workplace, and allowing the child who was harmed *in utero* to sue her mother. These four examples correspond to the four stages during which the state can act to prevent prenatal harms: during delivery, during pregnancy, before conception, and after birth.

Mandating Cesarean Sections

The cesarean section is a surgical technique that is widely available and generally accepted in this country. In fact, of eighteen countries surveyed, the United States performs cesarean sections at the highest rate [169]. Many argue that the rate is too high, and concern about the incidence of cesarean sections has existed for years: In 1980, for instance, experts at a consensus conference sponsored by the National Institutes of Health agreed that physicians should work to reduce the rate considerably [166]. Yet the percentage of deliveries by cesarean section has continued to rise (to 22.7 per 100 deliveries in 1985) [225]. Certainly many of these operations are unnecessary [103]. However, the issue is not whether the procedure should ever be recommended – for most would agree that it is medically indicated in many cases – but rather, should it ever be required? That is, would a court of law be justified in compelling a pregnant woman to undergo a cesarean section against her will?

Chapter Two contended that a pregnant woman has moral obligations to accept certain burdens in order to prevent and/or avoid causing serious prenatal harms, and that there are sound reasons for holding that some of these moral obligations should be legal obligations as well. However, mandating the administration of surgical intervention would be justified only under very limited circumstances (if ever):

1) The woman is in the final stage of pregnancy (and so her duty of care is at its most stringent);
2) The harm to the child is a harm of great magnitude to a very important interest (i.e., it is either life-threatening or would result in a life of grave affliction);
3) The probability that the harm will occur without the intervention is very high, as is the certainty of the diagnosis;
4) There is a very high probability that the harm will be prevented (i.e., there is a very good chance that the fetus will survive the operation and that the operation will be a success);
5) The risks of harm to the woman are relatively minor;
6) All requirements of due process are met.

Chapter Three, on the other hand, offered a variety of arguments against adopting any policies that require pregnant women to act in the interests of their future children. Of these, one of the strongest is that coercing a pregnant woman to accept medical treatment against her will would be discriminatory insofar as such concessions are not required of other people, including the parents of ailing (born) children.

However, since parents are generally expected to provide some types of medical care for their children – and since the only way some serious prenatal harms can be treated is to invade the body of a pregnant woman – this issue requires further discussion. In addition, because this book is concerned not only with describing what is now the case but also with examining what should be the case, a reassessment of parental duties seems in order.

Requiring a Pregnant Woman to Undergo a Cesarean Section

A cesarean section in the case of acute fetal distress could fit most of the conditions listed above, but not all of them. The level of risk to the mother involved in a cesarean section, for instance, is far from minor. In fact, the costs to her of undergoing a cesarean section against her will are substantial, and include an increased risk of infection and even death (the risk to the mother's life with surgical delivery is several times greater than with vaginal delivery),[1] the discomforts of recovering from major surgery, and the negative psychological repercussions of having her judgment overruled and her body invaded against her will. The question for us is whether these costs are great enough to preclude ever requiring her to undergo the procedure.

The answer to this depends in large part on what costs we may reasonably expect parents in general to bear in order to protect their children from harm (recall that at this stage of pregnancy, a woman's duties to her future child approach the stringency of any parent's to his or her (born) child). It was mentioned earlier that a parent should act within a 'reasonable' range of meeting a child's basic needs. But would this range also include undergoing surgery for the sake of the child? We need to compare the costs parents in general should bear with the costs to a pregnant woman of undergoing a cesarean section against her will, in order to ascertain that we would not be requiring pregnant women to accept significantly greater burdens than anyone else; to do otherwise would be to discriminate unfairly against pregnant women.

At present, the law does not require parents to undergo bodily invasions for the sake of their children. But looking to the state of the law will not be of much help: Not only is there no consensus about the proper scope of parental authority – and past reliance on parental authority seems to be waning as children's rights are taken more seriously – but the law itself is properly open to moral criticism. In order to clarify our thinking, then, let us consider two hypothetical cases (the details of which have been designed to correspond as closely as possible to the case of a pregnant woman who refuses a cesarean section):

> 1. Ten year old Alex is dying of leukemia, and a transfusion of bone marrow offers his only chance for survival. The one compatible donor the medical team has been able to locate is the boy's mother, but she refuses to undergo the series of 150 punctures of the pelvic bone (performed under general anesthesia) necessary to

acquire the needed quart of marrow. The donor faces a very small risk of death from the administration of anesthesia, and considerable pain – as well as a small risk of infection – from the punctures. Her bone marrow would regenerate.

2. One year old Susan suffers from advanced liver disease, and she cannot survive without a liver transplant. Since approximately 50 percent of infants like Susan die before a donor organ becomes available, her physicians would like to use part of the liver of her father. Experience at this hospital has indicated that the donor's risk of death is very low, and that post-operative complications are less than 5 percent; the discomforts of recovering from the surgery are significant. With the transplantation, Susan's chances for survival soar from zero to 80 percent.[2] Her father, however, refuses to undergo the procedure.

These cases are similar to the cesarean section cases in that: a) a child will die unless certain medical interventions are performed; b) the medical interventions require the parent's cooperation; and c) this cooperation involves invasion of the parent's body.

What should the physicians in these two cases do? Should they ask a court to intervene to compel either (or both) of the parents to cooperate? Should statutes be developed requiring parents to undergo either (or both) of these procedures?

Those who answer 'no' to these questions – and I count myself among them – would no doubt also be loathe to require a pregnant woman to undergo a cesarean section against her will. It was argued in Chapter Two that a parent's duties towards his or her child are based in large part on the interests of the child, but they are limited by the interests and rights of others (including those of the parent). Thus parents are not legally obligated to do what is in the child's absolutely best interests, but rather they must act within some acceptable, reasonable range of these interests. And while parents are expected to sacrifice more for their own child than for someone else's, there must be limits on how great a sacrifice the state may require. Although we may want the parents in the two hypothetical cases to undertake the risks necessary to save their children's lives, and although we may regard them as moral cowards for not doing so, my guess is that most people would consider such sacrifices of autonomy and bodily integrity – with the concomitant pain and risk (albeit small) of death – to go well beyond the range of what should be legally required of a parent.

Those who believe that the parents in the hypothetical cases should be legally required to undergo the procedures need to examine other features of the cesarean section cases before coming to a conclusion about whether *that* procedure should ever be compelled by the state. One problematic aspect is the high level of certainty required. In obstetrics, mistakes are not uncommon,[3] and the unexpected does occur: Chapter One noted a case in which a woman's placenta previa seemed to correct itself, allowing the child to be born naturally. A New York case was perhaps even more dramatic. A hospital petitioned the court to order a thirty-five year old indigent woman to have a cesarean section because the umbilical cord was wrapped around the infant's neck and would strangle the child during birth, but the court refused to issue the order, and the mother gave birth naturally – to a healthy baby [133]. Indeed, with regard to the pregnant women who were ordered by a court to undergo a cesarean section, the statistics are rather startling: Of the first five women for whom courts mandated cesarean sections, only two underwent the operation; the other three were able to deliver live children vaginally [187]. The degree of uncertainty involved in many of these cases provides a strong argument for allowing a woman to decide what will happen to her own body.

Another problem is fulfilling the requirement of due process. Since many of these cases are treated as emergencies, a lack of time may preclude the adequate representation of the pregnant woman's interests, violating her right of due process. This is not merely an idle worry. In outlining their survey of court orders that were sought to override a pregnant woman's refusal of therapy, researchers noted that:

> In 14 of 20 cases (70 percent), hospital administrators and lawyers were aware of the situation for a day or less before a court order was pursued. In five cases (25 percent), they were aware for two to seven days, and in one case, for more than seven days. Once a court order was deemed necessary, it took six or fewer hours to obtain it in 14 of 16 cases (88 percent). In three of these cases (19 percent), the court orders were actually obtained in an hour or less; at least one order was granted by telephone [125, p. 1193].

It is scandalous that a court would order the violation of a woman's body against her will after only a telephone conversation. And in fourteen cases, courts were able to decide within six hours of being contacted that invasive medical treatment should be imposed on unconsenting women. How thoroughly could the women have been represented on such short notice? Given the fundamental importance of the women's interests at stake in these cases, and given that they had no prior knowledge that medical treatment might be imposed – since there are no statutes, no well-known common law precedents, no administrative regulations to that effect – it is disgraceful that the courts would act so quickly to overrule them, and that they would have no appeal. This is not what is meant by due process.

Should the policy be altered? Should pregnant women be given notice that cesarean sections may be imposed upon them against their wills? No.

The death of any term fetus is certainly tragic; and the death of a term fetus who could have been saved is a very high price to pay for 'protecting the rights of all competent adults, and preventing forcible, physical violations of women by coercive obstetricians and judges'[10]. But while I would argue that a woman is morally obligated to undergo a cesarean section in order to save the life of her term fetus, I do not believe that the state should have the power to force her to do so: The state should not be able to override completely one person's interests in privacy and bodily autonomy in order to save the life of another. This is a sad resolution of a heartbreakingly difficult dilemma, but unfortunately there is no better option: The alternative would shatter too many important moral and legal rules and would involve an unacceptable increase of discretionary state power where the potential for abuse is high.[4]

Legally Compelling Parents to Undergo Less Invasive Medical Procedures

The determination that a cesarean section should not be legally required does not imply, however, that no medical interventions may be legally required. The claim that a parent may always refuse to undergo even the most minor of bodily invasions and thereby lose the life of his own child seems to me to be intuitively wrong. Perhaps other less invasive and less risky procedures would be more commensurate with the standard of care that may be legally required of parents (including pregnant women).

The idea here is that, while the state may not order a parent to undergo major surgery for the sake of his child – for this would totally defeat the parent's interests in bodily integrity and privacy – the state may sometimes be justified in setting back those interests to a lesser degree in order to obtain a very important good (such as saving the life of a child or a term fetus). Perhaps a line can be drawn between permissible and impermissible legal requirements, based on the degree to which an important interest is set back. (As Chapter Two mentioned, slightly thwarting an interest is easier to justify than down-right defeating it). Under some circumstances, then – assuming the requirements of due process and proportionality discussed earlier are met – it may be justifiable to require a parent to undergo minimally burdensome procedures, such as those involved in taking blood, in order to save the life of his or her child.

But although this may appear to be a small price to pay for the life of a child, we should be very cautious about concluding that it should always be legally required. The religious convictions of some parents, for instance, compel them to refuse any and all medical treatment. While I would not argue that respecting a parent's religious beliefs is more important than preserving the life of his child – and so I agree that the state should intervene to require medical treatment for a (born) child whose life would otherwise be lost – I do think that respect for the parent's religious beliefs buttresses the case for not requiring him to undergo a medical procedure in order to save the life of his child: His right of bodily integrity would still be invaded (albeit only to a minor degree), while his rights of privacy and parental authority and his right to follow the tenets of his religion would be trampled on. The combination of factors in this case, I believe, militate against legal coercion. Thus I would also argue against requiring a pregnant Jehovah's Witness to accept blood products.[5] Under some circumstances, then, a parent (or a pregnant woman) should be free to refuse to undergo even a minor medical procedure needed to save the life of his or her child.

Given the nuances and complexities of the issues, I doubt that these cases could be addressed adequately through any type of general ruling.[6] Thus I suggest that the question at hand – whether a parent (including a pregnant woman) should ever be coerced by the legal system into undergoing a relatively non-invasive form of medical treatment in order to save the life of his or her child – should be dealt with on a case-by-case basis. And I agree with the conclusions of the Committee on Ethics of the American College of Obstetricians and Gynecologists [53] that court involvement with treatment decisions should almost always – but not always – be avoided:[7]

> 1) With the advances in medical technology, the fetus has become more accessible to diagnostic and treatment modalities. The maternal-fetal relationship remains a unique one, requiring a balance of maternal health, autonomy and fetal needs. Every reasonable effort should be made to protect the fetus, but the pregnant woman's autonomy should be respected.
> 2) The vast majority of pregnant women are willing to assume significant risk for the welfare of the fetus, a problem arising only when this potentially beneficial advice [the physician's recommendation] is rejected. The role of the obstetrician should be one of an informed educator and counselor, weighing the risks and

benefits to both patients, as well as realizing that tests, judgments and decisions are fallible. Consultation with others, including an institutional ethics committee, should be sought when appropriate to aid the pregnant woman and obstetrician in making decisions. The use of the courts to resolve these conflicts is almost never warranted.
3) Obstetricians should refrain from performing procedures unwanted by the pregnant woman. The use of judicial authority to implement treatment regimens in order to protect the fetus violates the pregnant woman's autonomy. Furthermore, inappropriate reliance on judicial authority may lead to undesirable societal consequences such as the criminalization of noncompliance with medical recommendations.

Mandatory Treatment for Substance Abuse

Given that the state is not ordinarily permitted to require substance-abusing noncriminals to enter detoxification programs, it seems reasonable to assert that there must be a compelling state interest to warrant a change in the rules with regard to pregnant women. The obvious response is that the singular vulnerability of the fetus calls for extraordinary action on its behalf. The fetuses of substance-abusing women, like the children of substance-abusing parents, are at risk of grave harm. But while a variety of people – school teachers, day care workers, neighbors, social workers, relatives, friends – may notice the plight of these children and come to their aid, the fetus is unique in existing within and being solely dependent on its drug-dependent mother. No one can take the fetus away for a day or a week or a month while its mother goes on a binge. Thus in order to save the future child, it could be argued, the state must interfere with the activities of its mother by using its coercive power to require her to reside in a detoxification center for the duration of her pregnancy.

There are good consequentialist reasons for requiring addicted pregnant women to enter residential treatment programs. First, residential programs are more likely to be successful than out-patient programs: As out-patients, pregnant addicts continue to have access to and to use illicit substances [36, 89, 240], while inpatient programs allow closer monitoring of the woman's compliance with the treatment regimen. So even if she is not permanently weaned from the drug, at least her intake of it would be controlled for the duration of her pregnancy. Second, the cost of lifetime care of a seriously impaired child is considerably higher than the cost of a detoxification program of limited duration, so the savings to society could be substantial if the child is born healthy.[8] Third, breaking the mother's addiction will help the child after birth, since alcohol and drug abuse have been consistently associated with child abuse and neglect [15, 122]. And the mother herself will benefit since she will no longer be in thrall to a chemical. Finally, we have the appealing possibility of saving children who, due to their mothers' addictions, may otherwise suffer serious impairments or even death.

And a great many children may be at risk. It has been estimated, for instance, that the worldwide rate of fetal alcohol syndrome (which is characterized by growth retardation, facial deformities and central nervous system abnormalities) is 1.9 cases per 1000 live births [2]. In the U.S., where illicit drugs pose an enormous threat, approximately 11 percent of all newborns show symptoms of their mothers' drug use: approximately 375,000 affected infants each year [The National Association for Perinatal Addiction Research, quoted in 229]. And the problem is even more serious in some states (e.g., New York, California and Florida). A study of pregnant women in one Florida county, for instance, indicated that 13.3 percent had positive results on toxicologic screening of urine for illegal drugs [40]. While these figures are disturbing, they may not be telling the whole story, and the real figures may indicate an even larger problem. One expert in the field, for example, believes that 'substance abuse in pregnancy may be the most frequently missed diagnosis in all of obstetric and pediatric medicine' [37].[9]

Before we get too enthusiastic about improving the situation, we need to probe more closely the realities of the cases at hand. One very serious problem is the great difficulty of determining precisely the long-term effects of maternal substance use on the child. There are a variety of reasons for this: 1) Pregnant substance abusers often fail to seek prenatal care, especially during the early stages of pregnancy, so the progress of their pregnancies cannot be monitored; 2) of those who do seek health care, many lie about their use of teratogenic substances, so their physicians fail to look for that problem; 3) like most substance abusers, pregnant substance abusers tend to use a variety of illicit substances, making it impossible to determine the effects of any one of them in isolation and compounding the difficulty of treatment; 4) they frequently engage in other activities dangerous to their future children as well, such as smoking cigarettes and failing to eat properly [39, 96, 126]; 5) other influences – such as family socioeconomic status and family stability, maternal and child health, 'familial patterns of temperament, intelligence, or psychopathology,' must be considered when accounting for the condition of the children after birth [147]; and 6) follow-up studies on those children who remain in the custody of their mothers are difficult to conduct for the simple yet exasperating reason that the children cannot be located. In sum, the information we have about the teratogenic effects of substance abuse during pregnancy tends to be sketchy and tainted, and there is much more to be learned: When during the pregnancy does the damage occur (only at certain stages or throughout)? At what amounts are the substances dangerous? How permanent and severe is the harm? How important are other factors (such as the physical and mental health of the mother and the home environment of the child) in comparison? And why do some substance abusing pregnant women give birth to seriously impaired children while others do not? [1, 68].[10]

Since details (such as the degree and probability of harm) matter, we need to focus the discussion. To do so we will concentrate on the use of heroin during pregnancy, which has the advantage of having been studied for years.[11] Consider, for instance, the case of Margaret Reyes, which was described in the previous chapter. She was told to stop taking heroin, but she did not, and subsequently gave birth to twins suffering from drug withdrawal. Should stronger steps have been taken with her? Should she have been required to enter a residential drug treatment program until she gave birth?

Use of Heroin During Pregnancy

Chapter Two argued that the state would be justified in interfering with the activities of pregnant women only if there is a very high probability that major harms to the future child will be prevented. While much needed information about the effects of heroin use during pregnancy is still lacking, there is a considerable amount of solid evidence that heroin use during pregnancy may seriously damage the child while he or she is still *in utero*. One dramatic effect is drug-addiction of the newborn, which is unpleasant and even painful for the child, involving irritability, vomiting, diarrhea, insomnia, dehydration, sweating, and convulsions [90]. Hyperactivity, impaired attention span, and the effects of low birthweight are frequent long-term consequences [6, 65, 87, 239].[12] Consistent reports of these ill effects of maternal heroin use have been noted for years, and should therefore meet the level of reliability demanded. Would the risk of these harms justify requiring pregnant heroin users to enter treatment programs against their wills?

First, let us take a closer look at the potential harms and benefits at stake. Although investigators recognize a high incidence of behavioral problems among children of heroin addicts, there is no consensus regarding the cause: The problems may be due to drug exposure *in utero*, or they may be due to being 'raised within a drug milieu' [239]. Requiring a woman to abstain from using heroin while pregnant, therefore, may do very little to improve her child's chances of succeeding in school if she later returns to heavy drug use.

And the newborn's drug dependence – while unpleasant and disturbing – typically only lasts several weeks (although cases of its enduring for as long as four months have been recorded), and usually can be treated effectively [111]. Thus it does not constitute a serious enough harm to warrant state intervention.

The low birthweight of these infants, however, does involve risk of significant harm: Low birthweight children (under 2500 grams) are much more likely than normal birthweight children infants to have neurodevelopmental handicaps, congenital anomalies and learning disorders, and are almost 40 times more likely to die during their first month of life [21, 56, 151]. Should the state have the power to coerce pregnant heroin abusers into entering drug treatment programs in order to prevent low birthweight children?

If so, then perhaps the state should also intervene to prevent this problem in general. The idea of mandating drug rehabilitation for pregnant women, after all, is to protect the future children, not to punish the mothers.

According to the Institute of Medicine, among the 'principal risk factors for low birthweight' infants in the U.S. are the mother's low socioeconomic status, African descent, low level of education, unmarried status, and age (under seventeen or over thirty-four) [56]. Any one of these factors has a clear correlation with low birthweight; several together indicate a very high risk indeed – and poor, single, uneducated teenagers of African descent are precisely those at greatest risk of having low birthweight infants. Many of these females do not want to get pregnant, and of those who do, most wish to bear healthy children.

These facts point to the need for a variety of social interventions: providing sex and health education in schools, making contraception more widely available and more easily affordable, offering inexpensive and convenient prenatal care. But should stronger measures be taken as well? Should the state compel all females at high risk of bearing a growth-retarded child to take steps to reduce the risk? Should pregnant women, in other words, be legally required to seek prenatal care and to follow medical advice? [13] Instituting such a policy might significantly reduce the number of impaired infants, since 'lack of prenatal care appears to be a common factor to all severely impaired children' [239].

As Chapter Three pointed out, however, this strategy suffers from serious shortcomings. First, the doctrine of informed, voluntary consent – which is applied in the U.S.A. to all competent patients – would be abrogated in these cases, giving physicians an unacceptable degree of control over their patients' lives. Second, the intimate lives of anyone at risk of giving birth to a low birthweight child would be open to state inspection. This would include not only poor, unmarried, uneducated women – an already down-trodden group – but a large number of others as well: Also among those at high risk of having a low birthweight child are women whose deliveries are spaced close together, women who fail to gain weight during pregnancy, women who suffer from hypotension or hypertension, women over the age of thirty-four, and anemic women [56].

In addition, the response of the legal system could well be problematic. Under one possible scenario, the courts would be overwhelmed with cases involving women who are likely to bear low birthweight children, and judges will choose to invade the privacy and limit the liberty of these individuals to an extent not usually tolerated in times of peace. Under a more likely scenario, the state would use its coercive force to interfere with the lifestyles of those pregnant females of whom society already disapproves (such as heroin abusers) or who lack social status (such as uneducated, unmarried teenagers). One need recall only the parallel fact that the women compelled by courts to undergo cesarean sections to date tended to be poor and members of minorities [125].

Neither of these alternatives – oppressing a great many women or unfairly discriminating against a few – is acceptable. A more promising approach is to expand the social benefits available to these women and to offer them incentives to take advantage of them. This suggestion will be explored further in another section of this chapter.

A final strategy is to concede that use of the state's power to coerce pregnant heroin abusers into lifestyle changes – while overlooking other women who have a similarly high risk of delivering low birthweight babies

– is discriminatory, but at least this particularized discrimination has a rational basis. After all, this country's official policy is one of 'zero tolerance' for the use of the illegal substance. Why not, then, enforce the ordinary criminal drug possession laws against pregnant women, sentencing them to a sojourn in a residential drug treatment program?

The answer is that it is not likely to work. The problem is not the failure of addicts to respond to treatment if they are coerced into it: Coerced patients often do as well as patients who have sought treatment voluntarily.[14] The problem is that too many vital questions about the process of drug rehabilitation remain, especially with regard to pregnant women. Because of the power of the addictions, the prevalence of illegal drugs in some communities, and our insufficient knowledge about addictions, it is enormously difficult to break addictions. And with heroin addicts often abusing a variety of substances – cocaine, alcohol, cigarettes – all of which may be teratogenic, the challenge of providing comprehensive and effective treatment is increased. As a further complication, pregnant women have usually been excluded from hospital and community drug rehabilitation centers, so there is a serious dearth of knowledge about how best to treat them[15] – as well as a grave shortage of programs willing to treat them [205, 211, 229].[16] Before we could expect pregnant women to get treatment for their addictions, we first must guarantee that the help is there. And right now it is not.

Hence under present conditions – where the level of information about the harmful effects of most drugs is low, the level of uncertainty about how best to treat pregnant substance abusers is high, and the number of centers willing to treat pregnant women is woefully inadequate – the state would not be justified in requiring pregnant heroin abusers to enter residential drug rehabilitation programs against their wills. Providing treatment programs on a voluntary basis, and entreating pregnant women to participate in them, is certainly a reasonable alternative. The programs might help some women and their children in the short run, and might offer valuable information about treating addictions to help others in the long run.

This raises a very important question: What if future data indicate conclusively that heroin use during pregnancy causes severe and long-lasting damage to the developing organism, and that residential drug detoxification programs are successful in preventing these harms? In this case, the harms at stake are grave as well as permanent, affecting fundamentally important interests of the child; the agent of harm is the mother, and in ingesting the drug, she shows reckless disregard for the risk of harm which her conduct poses for the child she intends to bear; the harm to the child can be prevented only by interfering with an already illegal activity of the mother; successful methods for preventing this harm exist; fulfilling the requirements of due process does not appear to be problematic in these cases (they are not emergencies); it should be possible to draft a law addressing this special case that is neither unconstitutionally vague nor unduly open to abuse; we need not worry too much about instituting a policy which discourages drug-abusing pregnant women from seeking prenatal care, since they tend to forgo seeking prenatal care anyway; and finally, removing their addictions might help, rather than hinder, their bonding with their children. Together these facts offer strong reasons for coercing a woman who ingests heroin to cease this activity during pregnancy.

But such a policy exhibits a real bias with regard to pregnant drug abusers – certainly insofar as we allow other pregnant women with high risk pregnancies to conduct themselves as they wish, and insofar as we continue to refrain from prosecuting non-pregnant possessors of illegal drugs or at least continue to sentence them more lightly. While highly questionable, our intolerance of a pregnant woman's drug addiction – while allowing other pregnant women to cause similarly serious prenatal harms and other drug addicts to go free – might be justifiable on the basis of a greater social good. But this means that requiring pregnant heroin abusers to enter residential drug treatment programs would be appropriate only if we are certain that instituting such a program will prevent prenatal harms and will not in fact create more harm than it is intended to prevent. And it is not clear that these conditions can be met.

A variety of concerns are relevant here: A coerced denial of freedom may foster the mother's resentment towards the child and thus shatter the bonding that might otherwise occur; it may jeopardize other aspects of the woman's life (she may lose her home, her job, her other children if placed in a treatment center for several months); and pregnant addicts – fearing that they would be compelled to enter residential treatment programs and craving the freedom to pursue their habits – may be even less likely to seek medical care, perhaps thereby placing their offspring at even greater risk of harm. In addition, the timing of the coercion matters: If the woman is ordered to enter a drug treatment program during the early stage of pregnancy, she may well choose instead to have an abortion (after all, she is in the grip of an addiction); but if she is not required to enter a program until she is near term, it may be too late to do any real good, since considerable damage may have been done during the first few months of gestation. Finally, since not all pregnant heroin abusers give birth to seriously impaired children [36, 89], a policy of coercing all of them into entering drug treatment facilities would be open to the charge of unjustifiably limiting the liberty of certain individuals (i.e., those whose drug habits ultimately cause no significant damage).

These pros and cons are difficult to assess conclusively, given the dearth of relevant data. However, on the basis of what we know and what we can anticipate, it seems reasonable to conclude that pregnant drug abusers should *not* be coerced by the state into entering residential drug treatment programs: Such a policy would create more harm than good.

Does this mean, then, that our hands are tied? After all, these women are taking illicit substances to the detriment of their children. And certainly their drug addictions do not reflect autonomous decisions. Thus the prospect of limiting their liberty may be less troubling than the prospect of limiting the liberty of other pregnant women.

As a compromise measure, then, we should consider requiring those pregnant heroin abusers who are likely to cause significant harm to their offspring to participate in outpatient substance abuse programs – assuming of course that we have acquired the appropriate expertise in treating pregnant addicts, we have developed the ability to predict which children will be harmed, and we have created the necessary number of treatment centers. Although an outpatient program is less likely than an inpatient program to curb drug abuse, it does offer the woman a real chance to control her drug use. And using the coercive force of the state to back the policy puts pregnant drug abusers on notice that society will not tolerate the harm they cause.

The penalty for refusing to take part in the outpatient program could be a sojourn in a residential treatment facility. Since the purpose here is to prevent harm to the future person, not to punish the pregnant woman, it would make sense to avoid the distress of a criminal trial, the stigma of a criminal record, and the threat of jail (where little medical treatment is available). Rather than proceeding via the criminal justice system, then, a variation on the traditional civil commitment process could be implemented.

But civil commitment – even to an outpatient program – is still a denial of liberty; and the defiance of a commitment once ordered can be credibly enforced only by confinement to a residential treatment center, which is an even greater denial of liberty. Therefore strict principles of due process must apply: The woman's rights to counsel, to hearing, to proper notice, to trial, and to appeal must be respected. These procedures are obviously costly, especially in terms of the time involved, but they may not be suspended or abridged.

It should be noted that, since the illegality of the substance is not the controlling issue here – the issue is the fact that the mother is causing grave and irreversible harm to her offspring – pregnant alcoholics should be subject to similar coercion by the state.

The question now is whether the outcome would be worth the effort. Merely listing the elements of the process, for instance, is enough to imply that too much time might easily elapse to prevent harm to the future child. And either the adversarial nature of the legal process to which the pregnant women would be exposed or the prospect of participating in an outpatient treatment program (or both) may be enough to convince many pregnant women to avoid seeking assistance (such as prenatal care and nutritional support), to the detriment of their children. Yet that loss may not be offset by the gains of those who cooperate, since they remain in their home environments and so continue to be prey to the same temptations that induced them originally to become substance abusers.

Hence while the proposal to use the civil courts to commit pregnant substance abusers to outpatient rehabilitation programs is reasonable in principle – the proposal is reasonable, that is, once certain conditions of access, effectiveness, and prediction of harm can be met – in practice it may fail miserably. But then again, it may not, if used wisely and sparingly. That, however, is a very big 'IF'.

Reproductive Hazards in the Workplace

A variety of chemicals that are widely used in the workplace – lead, benzene, vinyl chloride, carbon tetrachloride, chloroform, carbon disulfide, fluorocarbon-22, carbon monoxide, mercury, dioxin – can be reproductive hazards. Exposure to some of these chemicals can harm the developing fetus directly (teratogenic damage), while others harm the parents' reproductive systems and so indirectly harm the fetus (mutagenic damage); and exposure to still others (lead, ethylene oxide and vinyl chloride) may cause both kinds of damage [44, 123, 202].

As a result, workers who participate in the manufacture of a number of goods - rubber, plastics, pesticides, nylons, gasoline, adhesives, batteries, pigments, pipes, laminates, bullets - may be at risk of some sort of reproductive damage. In response, many major companies have instituted fetal protection policies which bar women from working in certain jobs that involve toxic substances.[17] Although in some instances only pregnant women are prohibited from working with specific materials, another common policy is to prohibit all females between the ages of sixteen and fifty from working with substances that are believed to be reproductive hazards unless the women can prove that they are sterile.

Employers have a variety of reasons for excluding all fertile women from working in certain jobs. First, some substances can cause a great deal of teratogenic damage during the very early stages of pregnancy, before a woman knows that she is pregnant. Second, some substances can damage the woman's reproductive system itself, causing fetal malformations or death when she eventually conceives. Third, some companies respond conservatively to the indication of risk of harm: Although there is evidence that a certain chemical causes genetic damage, for instance, the evidence may be unclear as to when the damage occurs, so all women are barred from working with the chemical as a precautionary measure. And finally, companies often appeal to economic considerations and the asserted litigation explosion, claiming that they want to avoid costly suits brought by damaged children, and that only prohibitive expenses would serve to reduce exposure levels to the point at which there would be no reproductive risks.

Although the expressed intention of these exclusionary policies is to protect future generations from harm (and to protect the companies from economic harm), one of the effects is to exclude women from many skilled and lucrative jobs and either relegate them to more menial and lower-paying tasks or preclude them from working in certain industries.[18] The repercussions of these exclusionary policies are far from minor: millions of jobs would be closed to women.[19] Thus rules forbidding women to work in certain jobs raise the specter of sex discrimination on a large scale, as women are barred from a variety of positions simply because they have the capacity to reproduce, regardless of their plans to have children or their career goals.

The best solution to the problems created by the existence of reproductive hazards in the workplace is to remove the hazards and make the workplace safe for all workers. But companies claim that this is not always feasible. Thus there seems to be a basic conflict between two desirable but incompatible social benefits: preventing serious reproductive harms and providing equal employment opportunities for women. As with the imposition of fetal therapies, the choice is between causing harm to some women in order to prevent harm to their offspring, or permitting harm to befall children in order to avoid harming their mothers.

But there may be something else at issue here as well. Some commentators contend that the protection of future generations is not the only concern of employers, and that employers use the existence of reproductive hazards in the workplace as an excuse to continue unfair patterns of sex discrimination [186, 238]. One cogent charge is that if the type of job in question has traditionally been occupied by males, then it is much more common for women to be excluded than if the type of job has typically been filled by females – even if both types of job are shown to involve significant reproductive risk [238]. An example given to illustrate this disparity involves female operating room personnel who are exposed to significant levels of anesthetic gases. Although these substances have long been considered to be reproductive hazards [8, 13, 48, 124], women have not been excluded from the operating theater. This failure to exclude, it is suggested, obtains from the traditional acceptance of women in (at least some aspects of) medicine; so removing them from that arena would be very difficult indeed, and certainly more difficult than prohibiting other women from holding jobs that women have not traditionally occupied [238].

The force of this charge would seem to wane as more companies adopt fetal protection policies and jobs once commonly held by women – such as those involving the manufacture of semiconductor chips – are now denied to them [23]. Yet these policies too appear suspicious, since much remains unknown about the effects of these substances, and it is not clear that the risk of danger is serious enough to warrant banning women in general from working with them [34].

And even if the existence of reproductive hazards in the workplace is not used as a smokescreen to hide an insidious prejudice against women, it remains true that women are being excluded from working with substances that may cause reproductive damage while men – who are also susceptible to mutagenic damage – are not. And this fact demands scrutiny.

The issues, of course, have been pursued through the courts, with interesting results. Three U.S. circuit courts of appeals [266, 272, 311] have agreed to the reasonable proposition that, while fetal protection policies barring women but not men from working with toxic substances are discriminatory, they may be justified as a business necessity if the employer can demonstrate that: 1) considerable (i.e., not speculative although not necessarily conclusive) objective evidence exists to indicate that there is a substantial risk of harm to the potential offspring of female employees from their exposure to toxic substances in the workplace; 2) scientific evidence also indicates that the hazard does not apply to the offspring of male employees; 3) the program instituted by the employer is effective in obtaining the goal of preventing harm to workers' offspring; and 4) no other, less restrictive alternatives exist which would accomplish this goal.[20]

One important and problematic question raised by the criteria recommended by the courts is how strong the employers' burden of proof should be, since a high degree of uncertainty is a regular feature in dealing with reproductive hazards in the workplace [43, 202, 204]. There is a great deal that remains unknown about reproductive hazards in general: What substances do in fact cause damage to the offspring of workers? At what levels are these substances safe or unsafe to fetuses? What are the probabilities that damage will occur? Does the damage occur to the parent (and hence indirectly to the fetus) or directly to the fetus? Do the substances affect men as well as women? As the Office of Technology concluded in its 1985 report on reproductive health hazards in the workplace,

> What is known about reproductive health hazards is far outweighed by what is unknown: most commercial chemicals and physical factors have not been thoroughly evaluated for their possible toxic effects on reproduction and development. Much of the information on suspected reproductive health hazards, as with other hazards, is derived from animal studies, which present problems of interpretation in extrapolating to effects in humans [172, p. 7].

Improving this state of affairs is exceedingly difficult. The damage, for instance, may not be caused by a substance used in isolation, but instead may be caused by one ingredient within a mixture of chemicals - and we have no simple, effective method for determining toxicity for complex chemical mixtures [14]. In addition, the harms may have a multitude of contributing causes that are impossible to isolate. Or the harms may be the result of cumulative or synergistic influences, each individual instance of which goes unnoticed.

Furthermore, the difficulty of assigning probabilities to one potentially harmful factor among many will remain a serious problem, since experiments designed to isolate one variable while controlling others may themselves be unethical. An experiment designed to determine the level at which a particular substance is harmful would be unethical, for example, because it would deliberately expose people to substances known to increase the probability of harm, presumably in doses large enough to be able to determine the degree of the probability. In other words, the experiment would involve intentionally harming innocent people. So the uncertainty involved in ascertaining reproductive hazards in the workplace seems to be as intractable as it is pervasive.

Nonetheless, decisions must be made, and made under conditions of real uncertainty. This requires reliance at least in part on informed guesses and intelligent assumptions. One assumption that underlies the policies at issue - which exclude women and not men from working in certain jobs - is that the risks of harm befall the reproductive systems of female employees to a much greater extent than that of male employees. This assumption, however, is highly questionable. Some industry analysts argue for a different conclusion; they contend that both men and women are at risk of harm. As a former director of the National Institute of Occupational Safety and Health wrote to the B.F. Goodrich Company,

> We must stand firm on the principle that if an exposure is sufficiently toxic to produce genetic damage in an unborn child or in a fertile female, then it must be considered to be equally toxic to the fertile male worker and to his unborn child....There is *a priori* no reason to believe that the genetic material of a male worker is in any way more resistant to toxic occupational injury than that of the female [24, p. 30].

And the evidence fails to support any conclusion that men are not as susceptible to reproductive damage as women [172]: There is growing evidence, for instance, that paternal exposure to certain substances in the workplace may lead to increased rates of still-birth, preterm delivery, and growth retarded newborns [204]. In addition, although there are many studies which purport to show that reproductive hazards to women do exist in the workplace, a large number of them are deficient both in design and execution [152, 226]. And since most studies are conducted on women and not on men, too little evidence exists to indicate the level of risk to the offspring of male workers.

This brings us back to the set of criteria suggested by the courts' doctrine of business necessity. An employer may be able to meet the first two tests – which do not demand conclusive proof nor require a consensus – simply because there is a plethora of data (albeit of varying quality) on reproductive hazards to women and a dearth of data on reproductive hazards to men. Thus men may continue to be exposed to reproductive hazards in the workplace simply because reliable data are lacking. This, needless to say, is an unacceptable basis on which to make such an important decision.

Meeting the third standard – that the exclusionary policy is effective in preventing harm to workers' offspring – is even more problematic. Some substances cause genetic mutations to both men and women, which may have deleterious effects on many future generations. If a particular substance negatively affects the reproductive systems of men as well as women, then a program which bars women alone from working with that substance cannot succeed in preventing harm to offspring because children will still be harmed through their fathers. Since such a policy would be ineffective, the reason for thwarting women's interests – preventing reproductive harm – is lost. And with it goes the reason for treating women differently from men.

In addition, we should not underestimate the extent to which women's interests can be seriously undermined by policies prohibiting them from working in certain jobs. The fact that some women have chosen to be sterilized in order to keep their jobs indicates the importance of these positions to them [16, 186].[21] By now, women should be taken seriously as vital and regular members of the workforce: almost half of all U.S. employees are female, almost 60% of all women work, and over two-thirds of mothers with children under eighteen are employed [31, 94, 231]. Denying these women equal participation in the workforce – barring them from jobs and relegating them to low-paying jobs – not only may violate their rights, but may harm them and their children. The consequentialist claim that we would do more good overall if we prevented harm to future generations caused by workplace hazards is true only if the benefits to these individuals outweigh the harm caused to them and to the women who wish to work in the jobs from which they are excluded.

This is not to suggest that any policy which excluded women and not men is unjustifiable. Such a policy may be acceptable, but only if it can be shown that a particular substance causes serious reproductive harm through the mother and not through the father. Yet while it may be reasonable to exclude at least some women and no men under these circumstances, it does not follow that it would be reasonable to exclude all women from working with that substance. Simply because a woman is fertile does not mean that she intends to reproduce: Some women are celibate, some are gay, some use birth control, some would get abortions. Further, many women who are of child-bearing age, and believe themselves to be fertile, are not. And some desperately need the money offered by the riskier jobs in order to care adequately for their families. To treat all fertile women (or all who are presumed to be fertile) as though they were potential mothers – and ignore the relevant differences in their goals, needs, lifestyles and responsibilities – is to demean them, to deny them not just the right to equal employment opportunities but also the right to be rational adults, to weigh their risks and obligations as they see fit.

This brings us to an argument against permitting any fetal protection policy that excludes at least some women and no men. Thomas Murray reminds us of the unfortunate reality that morally responsible parents may sometimes have good reasons for exposing their children to risk of significant harm.

> Near the medical school in Galveston is a massive collective of petrochemical plants in a community known as Texas City. Texas City is a 'cancer corridor' – people who live there have a statistically higher risk of developing cancer than those who live in neighboring towns, presumably because of their proximity to the plants and their emissions. Suppose a man living elsewhere were offered a higher paying job in Texas City. Accepting it and living there would mean exposing himself and his family to a low but still increased risk of cancer. But it would also mean a higher standard of living for them all, better schools, and other advantages.
>
> Would we say of a man who accepted that job that he has done something morally wrong? Should we deny jobs in Texas City to men and women with children on the grounds they are exposing their unconsenting offspring to the risk of harm? [161, p. 20].

Those who believe that this man would be wrong to accept the job in Texas City – who believe that parents in general should never expose their children to risk of serious harm – could consistently hold that a woman who intends to bear children would be wrong to accept a job working with vinyl chloride or methotrexate. But they would also have to agree that many other desirable and socially valuable positions should not be given to men or women who have or intend to have or can have children. Some jobs – such as administering anesthesia – carry the risk of reproductive harm, while others – such as cutting timber and conducting police drug busts – carry the risk of orphaning the children of those who engage in them.[22] Were we to be consistent, we would have to agree that these positions, with their inherent risks of serious harm to children, should be given only to adults who do not have and who do not intend to have children.[23]

But is this conclusion really tenable? Adopted as public policy and consistently applied, this position could cause a great deal of social disruption, not the least of which would involve a drastic rise in the unemployment rate as well as a severe reduction in many useful commodities. A more realistic stance would be to recognize the sad reality that, like the man who moves his family to Texas City, parents often have to make difficult choices among imperfect options. The choice between accepting a decent-paying albeit risky job in order to support your family and working in a lower-paying job in order to avoid all risks of reproductive harm – when what you really want is the chance to earn a good salary without risking harm to your children – is a tragic choice. And some individuals' options are precisely so constrained: They do not have the freedom to take another job (since no other jobs for which they are qualified exist nearby); they do not have the freedom to move elsewhere (since they are held to the location by family obligations); and they do not have the freedom to stop working (unless they are willing to go on welfare). The choice here is between different sorts of responsibilities – responsibilities to one's present family versus responsibilities to future additions to one's family – both of which cannot be satisfied. I see no reason to conclude that choosing to act in the interests of the present members of one's family is in any way a morally blameworthy choice.

In addition, working in a job which carries a small risk of reproductive harm may be preferable in many ways to the available alternatives. As Judge Cudahy pointedly asks (in his dissent in *U.A.W. v. Johnson Controls* [272, p. 902],

> What is the situation of the pregnant woman, unemployed or working for the minimum wage and unprotected by health insurance, in relation to her pregnant sister, exposed to an indeterminante lead risk but well-fed, housed, and doctored? Whose fetus is at greater risk?

Thus it seems quite plausible to posit that a woman may be acting in a morally responsible manner when she chooses to work in a job that carries a small risk of reproductive harm. To deny her this morally acceptable option – to further limit her already constrained freedom to choose – is to deny her too much, and to discriminate against her unfairly. The decision, then, should be hers to make.

With this conclusion, the need to make workplaces safe for everyone takes on a new urgency.

Responding to Prenatal Harms after the Fact

The possibility of responding successfully to impaired children after their birth is an important issue, since conclusions regarding appropriate actions during pregnancy would be affected profoundly if we believed that some of the legal and ethical problems of pregnancy could be addressed more successfully after pregnancy.

In some states, any newborn whose urine test is positive for legal or illegal drugs is considered by law to be a victim of child abuse, and hospitals are required to alert local child welfare agencies. In other states, affected newborns are considered to be at high risk of being abused or neglected in the future, so they too are reported to child protective agencies. As a result, many drug affected newborns do not leave the hospitals with their mothers, but instead are placed with another relative (such as a grandmother) or in a foster home.

Whether or not an infant is released to its mother's custody depends in large part on others' perceptions of the mother's fitness to care her child. Not all drug-exposed newborns are separated from their mothers, of course; not all drug-abusing women are judged to be incompetent parents. But a woman with many years of drug abuse who has not entered a drug treatment program, who has shown no signs of attempting to deal with her addiction or properly nurture her other children, and who gives birth to an addicted child, is likely to leave the birth facility alone.

The concerns raised by removing newborns from their mothers are not fundamentally different from the problems confronted every day by child welfare workers who respond to evidence of past child abuse or neglect and who try to predict and prevent future cases, and by parents who face losing custody of their children. Since procedures and standards for removing children from their parents have been widely debated, and there is an impressive array of current literature on the subject [32, 58, 73, 129], the issues involved need no further exploration in this book. Instead, we will investigate a relatively new and untested way of responding to prenatal harm after the fact: expanding the realm of private law to allow children to sue their parents for having caused them harm while *in utero*.

Legal Suits to Remedy Prenatal Harms

Rather than allowing the state to intervene in the lives of pregnant women in order to prevent prenatal harms, we might do better to permit children who are harmed *in utero* to sue their parents later. Conceivably, invoking the private law might well have as much deterrent effect on the injurious activities of pregnant women as would invoking the criminal law, with the added benefit of providing compensation for the impaired child. In addition, the tort approach would be superior to the other methods examined. Unlike proposals to require pregnant women to behave in certain ways, the tort approach is immune to the disapproving charge of unfair discrimination against pregnant women, since fathers too may be sued. Recent evidence that a father's alcohol consumption may reduce birthweight in his offspring [136], for instance, could support suits brought by impaired children against their fathers. And unlike the use of criminal sanctions, tort remedies avoid the negative consequences of jailing mothers and branding them with criminal records. Tort law, then, may be the best method for dealing with these situations.

It was mentioned in Chapter One that prenatal negligent acts or omissions which show up as injuries later are widely accepted as legitimate causes for civil legal action. That is, courts recognize claims made for compensation on behalf of children who suffered unwarranted prenatal injuries and were born alive. Although some jurisdictions recognize as prenatal harms only those injuries inflicted on a viable fetus who is subsequently born alive, most courts allow claims to be made on behalf of a person who was injured at any point during his fetal period. And according to some courts, a person may even be harmed by events that occurred before he was conceived.[24] The harm in these cases is considered to befall the child, not the fetus, as Leonard Glantz explains:

> In compensating those infants who have been harmed as the result of prenatal injuries and were born alive, the courts have implicitly found that the true damage is suffered after birth, i.e., having to go through life with some defect or deformity. Thus, the damage has not actually been suffered by the viable or non-viable fetus,

> but by the human being who must now live with the handicap caused by the tortfeasor [101, p. 36].

One significant conclusion to be drawn from this brief review of the courts' treatment of prenatal harms is that the fetus as such need not be considered to have any moral or legal standing in order for the courts to recognize a prenatal harm, since it is the person after birth who actually suffers.

The type of private law response to prenatal harms with which we are concerned here is a straightforward tort suit: the child who had been harmed while *in utero* sues the person who negligently caused the harm.[25] As with other torts, there are four necessary elements to suits involving prenatal harms: 1) the defendant had a duty of due care to the child; 2) the defendant's act or omission was negligent; 3) the child was harmed (made worse off than he otherwise would have been); and 4) the negligent breach of duty was the proximate cause of harm to the child.

Several commentators have suggested that it would be appropriate to allow children to sue their parents to recover for prenatal negligent acts or omissions which later show up as injuries [171, 207, 215]. The proposal is that, rather than trying to prevent prenatal harms by using the threat of criminal punishment to coerce a pregnant woman into behaving in certain ways, we should instead provide a structure for compensating her child for any prenatal injuries she may have caused. Before we can conclude that allowing children to sue their parents for prenatal injuries is good policy, however, we first must explore the relevant countervailing considerations. There are two types of objections: 1) arguments against allowing children to sue their parents in general, and 2) arguments against allowing children to sue their parents specifically for prenatal harms.

Allowing Children to Sue Their Parents

For the first half of this century, American courts generally were persuaded that children's suits against their parents should not be recognized, believing that such suits would have seriously detrimental effects on the parent-child relationship [52]. Courts feared that, by allowing children to sue their parents, the state would thereby officially sanction the blame that children may place on their parents, and thus would create a means for destroying the family relationship – a relationship the state usually seeks to encourage and protect. Similarly, courts worried that recognizing such suits would undermine parental authority and control over their children, and that easy availability of a legal remedy might encourage people to go too quickly into an adversarial arena rather than attempting in good faith to work out their differences between themselves.

But while these are legitimate concerns, there are good reasons to believe that they should not be determinative. One reasonable response is that the courts misplace the responsibility for the disintegration of the family: It is not the legal system's recognition of legitimate claims for compensation that creates difficulties within a family, but the other way around – that is, the existence of serious family strife leads one member to seek compensation from another through the courts. In one of the first cases brought by a child against his or her parent, for instance, a daughter sued her father to compensate her for injuries suffered when he raped her; but the court rejected her claim in the interests of preserving domestic harmony [294]. It is difficult to see the logic of the court's response to this tragic situation, for it should be clear that an already troubled family will not be saved by denying one member legal remedy for harms inflicted by another.

A different type of argument against recognizing suits brought by children against their parents is that the children would not really benefit. Parents usually care for and support their children; if money were taken away from them and put into a trust fund for the child, for instance, the parents would have less to spend on the child, and the child's care might suffer thereby. Harming the plaintiff in order to 'compensate' him for his injuries clearly makes no sense.

It does not follow from this, however, that children should not be allowed to sue their parents. It simply means that these matters need to be decided on a case-by-case basis, and monetary compensation awarded only in those cases in which it will benefit the child. In addition, a sharp distinction is usually drawn in tort law between the question of liability and the question of ability to pay. For instance, minor children above a certain age can be sued, even though they usually have very shallow pockets and even though their parents are not generally liable for what they do.[26]

There are instances, of course, in which the plaintiff child might benefit monetarily from the suit: A trust could be set up for the child, and the amount of money the parent is compelled to make available for the child's support through the trust might be considerably more than the parent would spend on the child had there been no court award. But this too might backfire insofar as it could create enormous practical difficulties with regard to the child's care should the child remain with his or her parent, since a guardian *ad litem* would have to be appointed by the court to oversee the expenditures from the trust. Would the guardian be expected to select and purchase the child's clothes, for example, or simply pay for the clothes the parent selects? Would the guardian be expected to oversee the child's diet and schooling and extracurricular activities? The guardian *ad litem*'s responsibility for making the support decisions would no doubt infringe in some substantial ways on the parent's autonomy over his or her child, increasing the chances of a further rift between parent and child.

These types of cases raise another sort of concern as well: Some courts have worried that recognizing claims brought by children against their parents would create a means for defrauding insurance companies. As one court noted, 'We all know that realistically such actions are never thought of, let alone commenced, unless there is an insurance policy' [265, p. 150]. And another court added that, 'A parent [with liability insurance coverage] may encourage his minor child to bring such an action against him' [256, p. 417]. In order to protect against such fraudulent claims, some courts have decided to deny all suits brought by children against their parents. This could perhaps best be characterized as the throwing-the-baby-out-with-the-bath-water theory of case disposition, and it could be applied equally well – with obviously disastrous consequences – to many other types of liability insurance cases.

Courts have been moving away from the doctrine of parental immunity, however, and are recognizing a large range of suits brought by children against their parents; indeed, the majority of states have either abandoned or severely restricted parental immunity [18]. In addition to the reasons given above, this change of attitude has been motivated by the recognition that to deny a cause of action by children against their parents is to discriminate unfairly against the children. A related reason involves a concern for consistency in the law: Since courts recognize contract and property disputes between children and their parents, it seems reasonable to recognize torts as well. As one court noted, '[I]t is difficult to argue that the law should protect the property rights of a minor more zealously than the rights of his person' [261]. Thus most U.S. courts now seem to hold that there is no convincing reason – either of logic or of policy – to prohibit children from suing their parents.

Allowing Children to Sue Their Parents for Prenatal Injuries

One argument in favor of allowing children to sue their parents for having negligently caused them harm while *in utero* is that our society already recognizes prenatal harm in general as a legitimate cause for legal action, so it is unfair to prohibit a tort to go forward on the grounds that the alleged tortfeasor is the parent of the injured party. To do so would be to deny equal protection of the law to the person who has been harmed (unless there are compelling reasons for excluding parents from the class of wrongdoers).

In addition, the knowledge that children are allowed to sue their parents for prenatal harm may deter some parents from acting in ways that are likely to cause harm, while still allowing the parents the freedom to choose for themselves (unlike the coercive measures discussed above). Of course, the deterrent effect would not always exist: It is not likely that the possibility of a legal suit by her child would stop an alcoholic pregnant woman from imbibing large quantities of alcohol or a heroin addict from continuing to use the drug during pregnancy. And in any case, the deterrent effect will only work where the woman is mentally alert and educated enough to understand the very idea of torts and lawsuits, so that this knowledge can prompt her to take suitable actions during pregnancy in order to avoid the prospect of a later court battle. Nonetheless, if we allow children to sue their parents, compensation can be provided to this injured group in at least some cases in which threat of legal action did not deter the parent from negligently causing serious prenatal harm.

Finally, this method escapes the charge of unfair discrimination, since in principle both sexes may be held liable for a prenatal negligent act or omission which later shows up as injury to the child. It is expected that mothers would be sued more frequently, since they have more opportunities for causing prenatal harm, but men too can cause prenatal harm. Take, for instance, the case of Pamela Rae Stewart, described in the previous chapter. Ms. Stewart was accused of harming her son by having intercourse with her husband while she was pregnant and failing to seek medical care after she started to bleed. It could be argued, however, that her husband was also responsible for the child's condition, since he participated in these events even though he was (or so the prosecution claimed) aware of the physician's admonitions.[27] Had the boy lived, he might have had a cause of action against both parents.

Thus the state could recognize a legal duty of due care on the part of both parents enforceable after birth in a tort action by the child. The concern raised here, of course, is that this would create an untenable burden on the pregnant woman, since even her most mundane activities – such as ingesting cough medicine or aspirin or taking an airplane trip or exercising vigorously – could cause prenatal harm. In recognition of this, reasonable standards of care are needed (such as those discussed in Chapter Two). When applied to the pregnant woman, these standards of care would involve refraining from acts which a reasonably prudent pregnant person would avoid when that person knows or, in the exercise of reasonable care, should know that such acts cause prenatal harm. The pregnant woman's duty would also extend to the provision of those benefits that a reasonably careful pregnant person would provide. Chapter Two argued that this standard would be different in some important respects from the standard applied to reasonably prudent parents in general (since the fetus exists within the woman's body), and that her duty would be more or less stringent depending on the stage of her pregnancy. Using such standards would free a woman from civil liability for having engaged in potentially risky conduct which the reasonably prudent pregnant person would pursue, as well as for having caused relatively minor prenatal harms.

However, the use of the private law to compensate victims of prenatal harms, while theoretically acceptable, is far from being a real solution to the problem of prenatal harms since it is likely to be applicable only to those few cases in which the child has access to enough money to bring a lawsuit and/or the parent has enough money to provide compensation. And the question of money raises another, even more problematic consideration: The 'deep pockets' elements of our tort system could well induce some child-plaintiffs to sue their mother's physicians as well as their mothers. In that case, obstetricians would have an incentive to become more coercive toward their patients – using the courts to compel pregnant women to accept certain treatments or to undergo certain lifestyle changes – in order to reduce their own long-range legal liability.

The Illinois Supreme Court found an additional problem with such suits: 'Mother and child would be legal adversaries from the moment of conception until birth' [300]. While holding a third party liable for prenatal injuries may make sense, the court asserted, holding a mother liable for similar injuries does not: 'No other defendant must go through biological changes of the most profound type...in order to bring forth an adversary into the world.' The court concluded that a child should not be able to sue her mother for having caused prenatal injuries – due to an automobile accident in this case – because such suits would infringe too much on the mother's rights of privacy and bodily autonomy.

There is one other countervailing consideration: A pregnant woman who fears that the child she intends to bear will eventually bring suit against her in court might choose instead to have an abortion. While this does not trouble everyone, it is enough to deter others from advocating the tort remedy. Illinois state Senator Richard Kelly, for instance, has stated that although a child ought to have the right to sue her mother for prenatal harm, he is unwilling to introduce a bill permitting such action for fear that abortions would increase as a result [146].

The risk of these unappealing side-effects militates against allowing children to sue their parents for prenatal harms, and provides us with yet another reason for seeking a less adversarial method for responding to the problem of prenatal harms. Indeed, all of the proposals we have examined have serious problems: They are either ineffective, unfair, or too costly (both in terms of their burdens on individuals and their negative social consequences). We remain, then, without a good legal solution to the problem of avoidable prenatal harms. There is no good solution. But there is a relatively unintrusive approach that ought to be tried: intensifying educational efforts, making contraceptive methods more available and affordable, providing free prenatal care, offering positive rewards for pregnant women who change their life styles, and so on.

Social Reform

The most effective and least coercive way to reduce the incidence of avoidable prenatal harms is to improve women's general quality of life, since social disadvantages – such as low socioeconomic status, lack of education, inaccessibility of prenatal care, and stress – significantly increase the risk of serious prenatal harm [56, 239]. The opportunities for improvement exist on many fronts. One commentator, for instance, argues that,

> The best chance the state has to protect fetuses is through actions to enhance the status of all women by fostering reasonable pay for the work they do and equal employment opportunities, and providing a reasonable social safety net, quality prenatal services, and day care programs [11, p. 14].

And another adds that,

> Guaranteeing pregnant women adequate food, housing, and medical care would go very far toward improving the health of the children they bear. Also, accommodating pregnancy in the workplace through paid disability leave, liberal parental leave for both parents, part-time employment, and flexible hours, all without hidden penalties on career advancement, would enable women to give more consideration to the health of their fetuses, as well as to their own health [119, p. 39].

These goals are laudable indeed, and accomplishing them would no doubt significantly reduce the incidence of prenatal harm and enhance the quality of life of many people.

Proposals for providing a comprehensive set of social benefits to women and children should be taken seriously. They are in some countries: In Sweden, for example, the government subsidizes day care centers and health care programs, and employers offer eighteen months of paid parental leave from work; and the citizens of the Netherlands enjoy an extensive social security net which offers financial assistance throughout their lives.[28] Although the U.S. is far from having a similarly generous network of support programs, it has continued to show at least a modest commitment to providing social services: Congress has consistently supported antipoverty programs (at least to the extent that it has not cut funding to these programs as deeply as it could have), and it recently widened pregnant women's eligibility for Medicaid benefits; the vast majority of Americans have some form of health insurance (either public or private); a variety of municipalities have passed comparable-worth laws (evening out the wage levels of male and female workers); more and more corporations offer leaves to new parents (with assurances of comparable jobs when they return);[29] the federal government (through its Social Services Block Grant) as well as many companies provide day care benefits, and so on.

Yet in some measure, of course, it is highly unlikely that this country will soon provide a secure social safety net under which its citizens need not fall, or that American businesses will become significantly more sensitive to the needs and concerns of parents. Certainly the necessary set of social programs will not be established soon enough to prevent the impairment of thousands of infants.[30] But recognizing that these benefits will be withheld is one thing; believing that these benefits should be withheld turns all declarations of concern for healthy babies and healthy children – and certainly all statements of concern for preventing prenatal harm – into empty (and suspect) pronouncements.

Given that major American social institutions will not soon be transformed, this country can at least increase its efforts to enhance some of its current programs. I noted above that one area in which there is considerable room for improvement is the treatment of pregnant drug addicts, and there are other methods as well which have the potential for greatly reducing the incidence of prenatal harm and improving the health of infants. Two will be explored here: improving women's access to medical care and nutritional support.

Medical Care

Considerable evidence exists that prenatal care is effective in reducing infant mortality and morbidity [56, 88, 105, 158, 160, 184]. While most pregnant women in the U.S. have access to prenatal care in theory – the majority of large and medium sized companies provide prenatal care as part of their health insurance benefits, while all state Medicaid programs cover prenatal care – in fact millions of pregnant women find it difficult to receive adequate medical care [4, 56, 167]. Those most likely to receive little or no prenatal care are indigent, unmarried teenagers of African descent; and these are precisely the individuals who are at greatest risk of having low birthweight babies [22, 56].

Some women do not receive medical care because they do not seek it: They are stymied by a lack of transportation, or an inability to find someone to care for their other children, or a fear of the medical establishment, or a lack of knowledge about the importance of prenatal care and/or the availability of services, or an unwillingness to cope with the inconveniences and long waits at many clinics [120, 180].

Many other pregnant women go without medical care because it is not available. In studying individuals' access to health care across the country, the President's Commission for the Study of Ethical Problems in Medicine and Biomedical and Behavioral Research noted a striking unevenness in the distribution of physicians:

> One witness noted that 51 of Mississippi's 82 counties have no obstetricians and 50 have no pediatricians. In addition, 105 of the 170 obstetricians in the state and 92 of the 159 pediatricians practice in just five counties. Although family physicians are more evenly distributed across the state, a disproportionate share of the

> pregnant women and children at highest risk, who could benefit from the specialized care that obstetricians and pediatricians provide, live in rural areas [183, pp. 81-82].

And in fourteen counties in Georgia, for instance, there was not one physician who provided obstetrical care to Medicaid beneficiaries [183]. This was due in part to a dearth of physicians in some areas, and in part to the reluctance of some physicians to treat Medicaid patients.

A poor pregnant woman's lack of access to medical care is not isolated to the South; approximately twenty-three percent of all physicians nationwide refuse to treat Medicaid patients. And specialists most likely to treat pregnant women and children are among those least likely to see patients who receive Medicaid benefits. A 1980 study indicated that over 24 percent of general practitioners refused to see Medicaid patients; almost 37 percent of specialists in obstetrics and gynecology refused; and over 24 percent of pediatricians refused [157] – and this widespread refusal of private physicians to treat pregnant Medicaid beneficiaries has not improved [4]. Compounding the access problem is the fact that even those Medicaid beneficiaries who have access to a physician may not receive adequate health care because of the limited benefits offered by the program [4]. In addition, approximately 17 million women of child-bearing age have no health insurance coverage for maternity care [4],[31] and these women too have considerable difficulty receiving adequate medical care [131, 241].

One result of the dearth of prenatal care is that many children are born handicapped who could have been born healthy. In one recent case, a woman who had not received prenatal care before delivery bore a child suffering from cataracts as well as liver and heart problems caused by her syphilis – all of which could have been prevented had she been given a $20 injection of penicillin. The child survived for a only a month, at a cost of over $70,000 for hospital care [167]. And the incidence of low birthweight (2,500 grams or less), which is a major determinant of infant mortality and morbidity, could be reduced significantly with adequate prenatal care. In its 1985 study on low birthweight infants, the Institute of Medicine concluded that,

> Efforts to reduce the nation's incidence of low birthweight must include a commitment to enrolling all pregnant women in prenatal care. Many of the women who now receive inadequate prenatal care are those at greater than average risk of

> a low birthweight delivery. Moreover, participation in a system of prenatal care is a prerequisite for many individual interventions that help reduce the risk of low birthweight.
>
> In reaching this conclusion, the committee reviewed carefully the data documenting the effectiveness of prenatal care and concluded that, although a few studies have not been able to demonstrate a positive effect of prenatal care, the overwhelming weight of the evidence indicates that prenatal care reduces low birthweight and that the effect is greatest among high-risk women. This finding is strong enough to support a broad national commitment to ensuring that all pregnant women, especially those at socioeconomic or medical risk, receive high-quality prenatal care [56, pp. 7-8].

The Institute of Medicine committee tried to calculate the cost of implementing all of their recommendations designed to reduce the number of low birthweight infants, but it was hampered by a lack of data. Alternatively, the committee decided to calculate the increased cost of providing high quality prenatal care throughout pregnancy to women who have the highest risk of bearing low birthweight children (welfare recipients with less than a high school education), and to measure this cost against the savings that would be gained (in hospitalization and ambulatory care costs) by a reduction in the incidence of low birthweight. According to the committee,

> The analysis showed that if the expanded use of prenatal care reduced the low birthweight rate in the target group from 11.5 percent to only 10.76 percent, the increased expenditures for prenatal services would be approximately equal to a single year of cost savings in direct medical care expenditures for the low birthweight infants born to the target population. If the rate were reduced to 9 percent (the 1990 goal set by the Surgeon General for a maximum low birthweight rate among high-risk groups), every additional dollar spent for prenatal care within the target group would save $3.38 in the total cost of caring for low birthweight infants, because there would be fewer low birthweight infants requiring expensive medical care [56, p. 17].

Private employers are also noting the cost-savings that prenatal care can bring. In 1984, for instance, the health care costs for the Oster-Sunbeam Company factory in Coushatta, Louisiana, totalled one million dollars – half of which went for the medical expenses of only four babies born prematurely. So in 1986 the company began a mandatory maternal education program and encouraged women to seek medical care early in their pregnancies. The effort has paid off so far: while the cost to the company per maternity was $27,242 in 1984, it was less than $3,000 in 1986 and approximately $3,500 in 1988 [97].

We should not lose sight of what really is at stake here, however. Not only would providing decent prenatal care save money, but it would also save lives and prevent a great deal of suffering as well.

Thus the medical benefits offered to pregnant women should be as comprehensive as possible. Admittedly this would require expanding the current system of benefits significantly, and thus spending considerably more money on prenatal care, but several programs have confirmed the value of this approach:

> Key reforms in such successful demonstration programs have included early, stable, and continuous enrollment; an expansion of benefits to include preventive health and patient support services as well as traditional medical and hospital care; adequate reimbursement; and extensive utilization of community-based providers skilled in caring for low-income patients and trained in the management of persons with medical and social risks. When such changes have been made, impressive results have followed, and sizable cost savings have been realized [195, p. 667].

An example is the Family Center Program, which has provided comprehensive prenatal and postnatal care of drug-dependent women since 1969 [89]. The program utilizes nurses, neonatologists, perinatologists, psychiatrists, and social workers in a 'team approach' to treatment. In addition to medical care and drug detoxification, the Family Center Program offers individual counseling, support groups, nutrition education, parenting classes and home visits. Although the program has had little success in keeping its patients from taking teratogenic substances – it is an outpatient program – it has had considerable success in reducing the incidence of low birthweight infants and premature births.

Of course, it is naive to think that simply making adequate medical care available to pregnant women would solve the problem of avoidable prenatal harms. There are many reasons a pregnant woman does not seek prenatal care, such as lack of transportation or babysitters, fear of physicians or ignorance about the value of prenatal care. Simply making the services available, therefore, would fall short of the goal of substantially reducing the incidence of prenatal harm. Hence supplementary public education programs are also needed, as well as incentive programs to encourage pregnant women to seek care. Money could be offered for each prenatal visit,[32] for example, and services – such as transportation to the health care institution and child care – could be provided.

If our society is serious about reducing the incidence of prenatal harm, serious enough to consider criminalizing some actions of pregnant women, then extending these benefits makes sense as a first step. Indeed, extending these benefits should be required as a first step.

Improved Nutrition

There is no doubt that maternal nutrition during pregnancy has an enormous impact on the health of the child after birth. Improper maternal nutrition may cause congenital malformations, may impair the development of the brain, and may produce low birthweight infants who have higher infant mortality and disability rates [54, 178, 196]. One fairly straightforward means of accomplishing the goal of increasing the number of healthier babies, then, is to increase the number of pregnant women who have adequate and appropriate diets.

The most common problem is presented by pregnant women who cannot afford a nutritious diet, and much is already being done to help them. In 1972, for instance, Congress revised the Child Nutrition Act to include the Special Supplemental Food Program for Women, Infants and Children (WIC), which provides supplemental food to low-income mothers with infants and to children below the age of six with nutritional problems. This program, which was implemented in 1974, has been successful in reducing the number of low birthweight babies and the number of newborns who require treatment in neonatal intensive care units, and has also been successful in reducing Medicaid costs [201, 206].

But much more remains to be accomplished. Many poor families either cannot obtain nutritional support, or receive a supply inadequate to meet their needs [193, 214]. There are many reasons for this: Some people live in remote areas and do not have easy access to social service agencies; some people are intimidated by the bureaucratic rules involved; some people still do not realize that these benefits are available. Many people, though, are poor but not poor enough to qualify for assistance, and this number increases as financial cuts in social services are made. Indeed, some studies have shown that, 'because of cutbacks in AFDC (Aid to Families with Dependent Children), food stamps, and the school lunch program, one third of the gains made against hunger and malnutrition in the 1960s and 1970s have been wiped out' [193, p. 92]. And cuts in other social service programs – such as housing subsidies and assistance with utility bills – leaves the beneficiaries with less money to spend on food. In addition, the WIC program continues to fall far short of providing benefits to all who are eligible [55]. As the Children's Defense Fund contends, 'The program is still underfunded and reaches only about three million people, or one-third of those who are eligible. Several hundred counties have no WIC program at all, and many other counties maintain waiting lists and have to turn away eligible mothers and children' [Children's Defense Fund, *A Children's Defense Budget: FY 1985*, quoted in 214, p. 151].

There is a different type of problem here as well: Some pregnant women have the means to obtain nutritional foods but eat badly anyway. Many of these women simply are not aware of what they should and should not be eating, and some of them would respond positively to educational efforts. But not all of them; it is surprisingly difficult to entice some pregnant women to change their eating habits [5, 192]. Reaching these women would involve more effort, such as offering individual counseling and reinforcement sessions. Although providing these sessions would be considerably more expensive than distributing pamphlets or showing films, the costs would be offset by the savings in neonatal intensive care [176]. Many low birthweight babies spend the first month of their lives in a neonatal intensive care unit, at a cost of approximately $60,000 each. For considerably less than this amount of money, a full-time nutritionist could be hired to counsel pregnant women regarding their eating habits. If only two mothers a year were persuaded to maintain appropriate diets, so two infants escaped the problems of low birthweight – and the cost of two months' treatment in a neonatal intensive care unit was thereby eliminated – the savings would be considerable.

There are some women, however, who would be deaf to the entreaties of a counselor. Take, for instance, the case of Adrienne Robinson:

> On a return visit to the hospital, Adrienne Robinson tells of how, three months pregnant, she began living alone in an abandoned car after her cocaine-smoking boyfriend beat here with a baseball bat, whipped her with an extension cord, and tried to move in another woman-friend.
>
> Ms. Robinson saw doctors once, after contracting pneumonia, then moved into a motel with another homeless woman, who hallucinated, beat her and traded Ms. Robinson's federal pregnancy-related milk and food supplies for cocaine. Ms. Robinson ate potato chips and smoked cocaine. 'I knew I was killing my baby, but I couldn't stop,' she says, rocking Christian, born with syphilis and cocaine addiction [167].

Although a counselor might have persuaded Ms. Robinson to change her ways, it is more likely that increasing food benefits to her would simply have improved her access to illegal drugs. Hence even stronger measures – such as intensive efforts to get her to enter a drug treatment program (assuming one is available) – might have been appropriate.

Discussion

It was argued in Chapter Two that pregnant women are morally obligated to refrain from behaving in ways that cause prenatal harm, and it was suggested that the state should sometimes intervene to ensure that they meet their obligations. But what would this mean for the pregnant women in the fifty-one counties of Mississippi or the fourteen counties of Georgia who cannot receive obstetrical care? If we as a society are so concerned about preventing prenatal harms, it makes more sense for us to ensure equitable access to basic health care services than to bring the coercive mechanisms of state criminal statutes to bear.[33] And providing indigent women with the means for obtaining nutritious diets would go further in reducing the number of low birthweight babies than would, for instance, committing drug-addicted women to jail (where they are more likely to receive the drugs to which they are addicted than they are to receive treatment for their addictions).

Making these benefits available would save the lives as well as improve the health of many children, without infringing on their mothers' rights of bodily integrity and private decision making. The existence of these less intrusive and cost-effective means of preventing prenatal harms stands as a strong reason against allowing the state to intrude into a pregnant woman's life in more invasive ways.

Conclusion

I have argued that, while a pregnant women has moral obligations to act in the interests of her future child throughout her pregnancy, there are compelling reasons against legally requiring her to meet certain standards of due care before it is uncontroversially clear that she will bring the pregnancy to term. Hence the state would not be justified in intervening to prevent some very troubling prenatal harms because they are caused during the early stage of pregnancy.

However, there still may be instances in which the state's interests in preventing prenatal harms may be strong enough to warrant overriding a pregnant woman's freedom of choice (which, after all, is not unlimited, even in principle) when it is uncontroversially clear that she will go to term. But an intervention would have to meet certain fundamental tests before it would be justifiable: 1) the harms to be prevented to the future person are grave and irreversible; 2) the harm to the mother is relatively minor; 3) the intervention involves the least intrusive means available, 4) the intervention will be successful in preventing or at least ameliorating serious prenatal harms, 5) requirements of due process and equal protection of the law are met, and 6) the benefits of adopting this type of state intervention as social policy will greatly outweigh the disbenefits.

There are, however, a variety of countervailing considerations: A woman's fundamental rights of bodily integrity and private decision making should not be subordinated to the welfare of someone else; state intervention into the activities of pregnant women will have seriously negative consequences (pregnant women will be unwilling to be candid with their physicians, for instance, or they will not seek prenatal care at all); a few reasonable limitations on the activities of pregnant women will lead inevitably to many unjust and onerous limitations (the 'slippery slope' arguments); it is not fair to demand things of pregnant women that are demanded of no one else in society, so requiring pregnant women to behave in certain ways or risk legal penalties is unfairly discriminatory; and it is almost impossible to draft fair, workable laws.

It is difficult at this early stage of the debate to evaluate conclusively the pros and cons of allowing the state to intervene in the lives of pregnant women in order to prevent prenatal harms. Good policy choices require reliable empirical data analyzing the consequences of institutionalizing the type of action in question, and many of the requisite sociological, historical, medical, and psychological studies have not yet been completed (or, in some cases, even undertaken). Arguments on both sides of the issue appeal to likely consequences, but no one really knows whether and to what extent these consequences will actually materialize. Hence my conclusions are necessarily preliminary and theoretical, and even a bit tentative. It does seem clear, though, that few, if any, coercive state interventions to prevent prenatal harms could meet the conditions stated above.

Although I have highlighted the substantial problems encountered in legally forcing pregnant women to act in certain ways for the sake of their future children, my analysis does not by any means imply that society should ignore the future persons who are (avoidably) harmed in the prenatal stage. There is considerable room for reform in the area between the extremes of instituting coercive measures backed by the power of the state – threat of criminal sanction, for instance, or direct court orders to undergo medical treatment – and giving pregnant women *carte blanche* to behave any way they wish.

Since many pregnant women in America cannot afford nutritious diets and have little or no access to adequate medical care or treatment for addictions, their chances are low of meeting acceptable standards of care toward their future children. If we as a society wish to require that people meet certain standards of due care, then we should make it possible for them to do so. And one real opportunity for compliance will come through improved social benefits: a method that can be expected to be more successful and less intrusive than using threats of criminal sanction or tort liability, forcing medical treatment or mandating drug detoxification. Hence before we consider initiating coercive state mechanisms to punish women who fail to maintain what we judge to be proper standards of care during pregnancy, we should at least give them a meaningful chance to do better voluntarily.

The proposal is, therefore, that we expand the level of benefits designed to promote healthy pregnancies: Increase the availability of prenatal care programs, offer incentives and inducements to women to enroll in programs designed to change behavior patterns, send out more social workers to educate women of child-bearing age, provide counsellors to attempt to persuade the more recalcitrant pregnant women to amend their ways, and so on.[34] And since those women who are pregnant even though they do not want to be are likely to fail to act in the interests of children they do not want to have, improving their chances of not getting pregnant would be an important step in the direction of reducing prenatal harms. Sex and health education in the schools should be expanded and required, and methods of contraception should be made more widely available and affordable.[35]

An increase in the level of social benefits will not be effective in eliminating all preventable prenatal harms, of course, and some pregnant women will continue to fall below the minimum standard of care of a reasonably prudent pregnant person. That most pregnant women love their babies is irrelevant; the fact of the matter is that some of them will negligently cause their children grave and irreversible harm while they are *in utero*. We should not pretend that these women are not responsible for the harms they cause; nor should society ignore its obligation to protect these children.

Hence I believe that the state may sometimes be justified in interfering with a pregnant woman in order to prevent prenatal harm. One suggestion, for instance, is that pregnant substance abusers, who usually are not in control of their lives, may be committed by courts to outpatient treatment centers (assuming certain conditions – of due process, access, efficacy, and ability to predict which addicts are likely to harm their offspring – can be met). I hasten to add, however, that given the considerable obstacles to administering any intervention fairly and well, the choices of the state should be very severely constricted. And I admit that I have yet to come across a case in which state intervention with the decision of a mentally competent pregnant woman to refuse medical treatment would be justifiable, although I do hold open the possibility that (at least) one exists. Finally, if our goal is to prevent harm to innocent children – not to punish their mothers – then providing more social welfare and incentive programs should be the first step; instituting coercive measures should be the last.

There is no good solution to the problem of preventable prenatal harms: Choosing the lesser of evils (which is the best we can hope to do) is still unsatisfactory, since one person's interests will be sacrificed for the sake of another's no matter what is done. At this juncture I cannot help but think of Karl Marx's statement that 'Mankind always sets itself only such problems as it can solve' [149]. Marx has been accused of being wrong about many things, and perhaps we should add to the list his belief in this assertion. I offer the subject matter of this book as an exception to his generalization.

Notes

[1] There are approximately 2.7 deaths per 10,000 vaginal deliveries, and 8-10 deaths per 10,000 surgical deliveries [59].

[2] While this procedure is still in the experimental phase, it is expected to have these parameters [216].

[3] For instance, physicians prescribed diethylstilbestrol (DES) to many pregnant women to prevent miscarriages, not knowing that it could cause cancer in their children. Diana Dutton [69] explores the reasons behind the widespread and 'uncritical embrace' of DES.

[4] Either a concern for upholding fundamental moral and legal principles *or* a concern about

the negative consequences of such a policy would be enough, I believe, to justify rejecting it; together, these elements seem compelling. For more on this subject, see [12, 86, 99, 118, 145, 168, 188].

[5] See Chapter One, Note 11.

[6] I am unable to formulate one over-arching general principle that would both uphold the relevant moral and legal principles and produce more good than harm overall.

[7] The Committee on Bioethics of the American Academy of Pediatrics came to a similar conclusion [7]:

> If a fetal intervention is one of proven efficacy and has concomitant low maternal risk, the physician should recommend the procedure and stress, if necessary, the responsibility of the mother to accept some personal risk for the potential benefit to her fetus. Should the woman refuse to undergo an intervention that poses a personal risk, her autonomous choice and risk to bodily integrity should, in general, be respected.
>
> In unusual cases, a physician may be unsympathetic to the woman's refusal of treatment. Under the following conditions a physician might consider actively opposing the woman's choice: 1) there is substantial likelihood that the fetus will suffer irrevocable harm without the intervention, 2) the intervention is clearly appropriate and will likely be efficacious, and 3) the risk to the woman is low. When these conditions are present, the woman's physician should inform her that the decision creates a moral dilemma for the physician and should try to persuade her to consent. If refusal persists, the physician may wish to inform the woman that he believes her decision is unreasonable and that consultation with a hospital ethics committee or others within the institution might be sought. Finally, in rare cases, recourse to the cours might be considered. Court intervention should be seen as a last resort to be undertaken with great caution because of the potentially regrettable consequences of forced medical or surgical procedures.

[8] One study estimated that the annual cost of treating some disorders associated with fetal alcohol syndrome – 'providing special services for pre- and postnatal growth retardation requiring neonatal intensive care, some specific organic disorders (e.g., cleft palate and hearing loss) requiring surgical repair and subsequent treatment, and mental retardation relative to FAS' – is $321 million in the U.S. alone [2]. The cost might be even greater in countries with higher rates of alcohol consumption by pregnant women. Studies show that approximately 70 percent of Danish women, for example, consume alcohol during pregnancy [173, 200].

[9] One study indicated that, 'the reported incidence of substance abuse in pregnancy rose with the increased thoroughness of the assessment utilized by the hospital staff and physicians.' Hospitals with a low level of assessment – in which pregnant women were not questioned about their drug use, and newborns were tested only if they exhibited symptoms of distress – reported a 3 percent rate of substance use; while hospitals with a high level of assessment – in which every pregnant woman and/or neonate was tested – reported a 15.7 percent rate of substance use (and several reported a 24 percent or higher rate) [37].

[10] Researchers justifiably complain about the 'overwhelming number of confounding prenatal and environmental influences and the small number of drug-exposed subjects who

have been carefully evaluated in a prospective fashion' [239].

[11] The use of cocaine during pregnancy, on the other hand, is a relatively recent problem, and there is no consensus regarding its teratogenic effects [38, 65, 68, 90, 96, 142, 144, 175, 242].

[12] Other teratogenic effects of heroin have been reported, but not consistently.

[13] Even more coercive measures are also available, none of which are advocated here. See Chapter Two, Note 7.

[14] Collins and Allison [50], for instance, conclude that, 'The evidence presented here suggests that the use of legal threat to pressure individuals into drug treatment is a valid approach for dealing with drug abusers and their undesirable behaviors. Legal threat apparently helps keep these individuals constructively involved in treatment and does not adversely affect long-term treatment goals.' See also [73, 148, 236].

[15] For instance, substituting methadone for heroin would not be enough to reduce the risk of harm to the future child if the mother continues to take other teratogenic substances, yet suddenly eliminating some of these drugs from the fetus's system (having it go 'cold turkey') may do more harm than good [126, 127]. And methadone itself causes damage to the fetus [38, 72].

[16] This problem is not unique to the United States. Researchers in Great Britain for instance, conclude that there as well 'Women's problems are not fully recognized and remain under-represented in treatment settings' [233, p. 119].

[17] Among the companies with fetal protection policies are Olin Corporation, Eastman Kodak, Goodyear, B.F. Goodrich, DuPont, General Motors, Johnson Controls, and American Cyanamid [23, 238].

[18] For instance, the policy at Johnson Controls' battery manufacturing plants, which has been in effect since 1982, states that no fertile woman can be hired for a job in which an employee has been found to have a certain blood lead level anytime during the previous year, or for a job which might lead to a promotion to such a job. In effect, this means that no production jobs are open to fertile women [272].

[19] Precisely determining the impact on women is exceedingly difficult, as Alan Blanco explains:

> A further estimate of potential impact can be made by considering the range of products processed with substances which form the basis of exclusionary policies. About 835,000 workers are affected by the OSHA lead standard, about two million workers are exposed to benzine, and hundreds of thousands of workers are exposed to vinyl chloride. Aggregation of these figures results in a very incomplete estimate of the potential exclusionary effects of fetal protection policies because the list of hazardous substances is very incomplete [24, pp. 763-764].

Judge Frank H. Easterbrook estimates that over 20 million jobs would be closed to women [272].

[20] In March 1991 the U.S. Supreme Court ruled that fetal protection policies are a form of sexism that is prohibited by federal civil rights law [272].

[21] For a discussion of the importance of work, the role of women in the workforce, and the value of 'good and fulfilling work' to the individual, see [100].

[22] Farming is also dangerous: In 1988, 140,000 agricultural workers in the U.S. suffered

disabling injuries and 1,500 died [62].

[23] Not only does the death of a parent frequently put the child at considerable financial risk, but evidence shows that the emotional damage to the child is often severe and long-lasting; indeed, the early loss of a parent may be instrumental in precipitating self-destructive conduct by the child years afterward [128].

[24] In *Renslow v. Mennonite Hospital*, for instance, the Illinois Supreme Court held that a child who suffered permanent disability to her brain, nervous system, and various organs had a legitimate claim for compensation as the result of the negligent transfusion of her Rh-negative mother with Rh-positive blood – over seven years prior to the child's conception. The court found that the child was harmed by the negligent transfusion because she was made worse off than she otherwise would have been, even though she did not exist at the time the harmful activity (the transfusion) occurred. The court reasoned that,

> The cases allowing relief to an infant for injuries incurred in its previable state make it clear that a defendant may be held liable to a person whose existence was not apparent at the time of his act. We therefore find it illogical to bar relief for an act done prior to conception where the defendant would be liable for this same conduct had the child, unbeknownst to him, been conceived prior to his act. We believe that there is a right to be born free from prenatal injuries forseeably caused by a breach of duty to the child's mother.
>
> The extension of duty in such a case is further supported by sound policy considerations. Medical science has developed various techniques which can mitigate or, in some cases, totally alleviate a child's prenatal harm. In light of these substantial medical advances it seems to us that sound social policy requires the extension of duty in this case [290, p. 1255].

See also [248, 275].

This reasoning is not universally accepted, however. In *Albala v. City of New York* [243], for instance, the court refused to recognize a cause of action brought on behalf of a brain damaged child whose injuries had resulted from a perforation of the uterus which had been suffered by the child's mother during an abortion performed prior to the child's conception.

[25] A complex variation on this is the 'wrongful life' suit; see [29, 33, 75, 85, 159, 222]. In a wrongful life suit, a child claims that, but for the conduct of another, she would not have been conceived or, once conceived, would not have been born alive, and that her being born with serious impairments (even though there was no possibility that she could be born without the impairments) was a harm that calls for compensation. The child states, in effect, that she never should have been born, and she claims damages for having to live with her permanent and severe handicaps.

The first 'wrongful life' suit was brought forward in 1963. In that case, the son of an unwed woman sued his father for creating his illegitimate state. The court refused to allow the child to recover, however, for fear that the judicial system would be inundated with suits brought by disgruntled children [312]. Most wrongful life cases, however, differ from this one in that a party other than the parent is the defendant (usually a health care professional), and the child's condition is worse than illegitimacy (for example, the child suffers from cystic fibrosis or Tay-Sachs disease). Nonetheless, many courts have refused to allow the children any recovery for damages, usually on the grounds that 'there is no rational way to measure non-existence with the pain and suffering of the child's impaired existence' [260] – and therefore there is no way to measure appropriate compensation for the child.

Other courts, however, have recognized that medical professionals may be liable for damages to children in wrongful life suits, although the damages awarded in these cases have not included pain and suffering awards but instead have been limited to medical expenses [255, 288]. And as a California court noted, wrongful life suits against parents may also be appropriate:

> One of the fears expressed in the decisional law is that, once it is determined that such infants have rights cognizable at law, nothing would prevent such a plaintiff from bringing suit against its own parents for allowing plaintiff to be born. In our view, this fear is groundless. The 'wrongful-life' cause of action with which we are concerned is based upon negligently caused failure by someone under a duty to do so to inform the prospective parents of facts needed by them to make a conscious choice *not* to become parents. If a case arose where, despite due care by the medical profession in transmitting the necessary warnings, parents made a conscious choice to proceed with a pregnancy, with full knowledge that a seriously impaired infant would be born, that conscious choice would provide an intervening act of proximate cause to preclude liability insofar as defendants other than the parents were concerned. Under such circumstances, we see no sound public policy which should protect those parents from being answerable for the pain, suffering and misery which they have wrought upon their offspring [255].

Notably, the California legislature responded to this case by enacting Civil Code Section 43.6, which ensures that children cannot sue their parents for bringing them into the world. And other states – including Minnesota, South Dakota and Utah – have passed laws prohibiting wrongful life suits in general.

In contrast are torts brought by the parents. Parents may sue a health care provider for 'wrongful birth' due to the provider's failure to warn them of the risks of birth defects or for giving them inaccurate information about the risks. The charge here is that the parents would not have brought the fetus to term had they realized its damaged state, and they sue for the expenses of caring for a seriously impaired child and compensation for their suffering in doing so. A similar type of case is 'wrongful conception' (also referred to as 'wrongful pregnancy'), in which parents sue health care providers over the failure of their attempts to avoid pregnancy (i.e., unsuccessful sterilizations, abortions or birth control measures) and the resultant birth of an unwanted child. Parents may also sue the person who negligently causes the death of a wanted fetus ('wrongful death').

[26] Some state statutes make parents liable for a limited amount.

[27] Criminal charges were not brought against the father because he denied knowledge of the doctor's recommendations and the prosecutor could not prove otherwise.

[28] Countries with generous social programs tend also to have high tax rates: Approximately 56 percent of Sweden's gross national product, for instance, is consumed by taxes (as opposed to less than 30 percent in the U.S.).

[29] However, maternity leave policies in the U.S. pale in comparison with maternity leaves in other industrialized countries: German workers, for instance, have fourteen weeks of leave at full salary, while French workers have sixteen weeks of leave at full salary.

[30] One problem is that the first step – raising sufficient funds to support these social benefits – will not be taken: few U.S. legislators are willing to propose something so unpopular as a tax increase.
[31] This can be explained in large part by the Medicaid programs' shifting and highly restrictive eligibility rules [195].
[32] It has been calculated, for instance, that were the Kaiser system – a large health maintenance organization in California – to offer a $100 incentive to each enrolled pregnant woman for seeking prenatal care throughout her pregnancy, the HMO would save millions of dollars annually in reduced hospital costs [160].
[33] An alternative view – one this book rejects – is that the only legitimate role of the state is to protect the negative rights of individuals, and this does not include the conferral of positive benefits such as health care. Proponents of this libertarian stance contend that the only social structure compatible with it is the competitive market, and all resources should be distributed by free market processes.

But there are serious problems with this position: The interplay of legitimate voluntary exchanges in the marketplace may lead to injustices. One countervailing consideration is that cumulative harmful effects on welfare and liberty created by unfettered market processes may be serious enough to provide strong ethical grounds for challenging the virtually unlimited right to private property and free exchange championed by libertarians. A second argument against the unchecked market is that because everyone has an extended period of dependence in childhood, how well one fares will be determined to a large extent by the voluntary exchanges of one's parents, not by one's own voluntary exchanges. A final argument against the libertarian position is that the market simply transmits the unfairness of the initial distribution of assets that people bring to the market. For all of these reasons, the moral and social costs of an unchecked market may be too high, and interference may be warranted in some circumstances.

Health care is frequently invoked as a legitimate exception to allowing market forces to operate freely. Using the ability to pay to decide which patients receive health care is, many argue, to discriminate unfairly against the poor, and need for health care should instead be the primary distributive criterion. This basically is the position assumed in this book – with the caveat that, because resources are finite and health is not the only good, not all health care 'needs' can be met.
[34] Some communities have already instituted such measures. In Washington, D.C., for instance, any pregnant woman whose annual family income is less than $20,000 can receive free prenatal care, and a van (the Maternity Outreach Mobile) is available to transport pregnant women to and from the medical clinics (as well as to remind them of their appointments).
[35] The Committee to Study the Prevention of Low Birthweight of the Institute of Medicine recommends that Title X of the Public Health Service Act be more generously funded in order to make contraception more accessible [56, p. 18]:

> Title X authorizes project grants to public and private nonprofit organizations for the provision of family planning services to all who need and want them, including sexually active teenagers, but with priority given to low-income persons. The committee urges that federal funds be made generously available to meet the documented need for family planning. The Title X program and family planning

services generally should be regarded as important parts of the public effort to prevent low birthweight.

It is important also to make more methods of contraception available. There are many highly successful methods used in other countries but not available in the U.S., such as the Filshie chip (which blocks the Fallopian tubes), Noristerat (a two-month injectable) and RU-486 (the 'abortion pill'). Examining these measures for possible use in the U.S. should be given a higher priority.

Bibliography

1. Abel, E.L.: 1984, *Fetal Alcohol Syndrome and Fetal Alcohol Effects*, Plenum Press, New York.
2. Abel, E.L. and Sokol, R.J.: 1987, 'Incidence of Fetal Alcohol Syndrome and Economic Impact of FAS-related Anomalies', *Drug and Alcohol Dependence* 19, 51-70.
3. Ahmann, S.: 1989, 'Mother to be Tried for Exposing Fetus to Cocaine,' *Ob Gyn News*, March 1-14, 1 & 26.
4. Alan Guttmacher Institute: 1988, *Blessed Events and the Bottom Line: Financing Maternity Care in the United States*, Alan Guttmacher Institute, New York.
5. Allen, C.D. and Ries, C.R.: 1985, 'Smoking, Alcohol and Dietary Practices During Pregnancy: Comparison Before and After Prenatal Education', *Journal of the American Dietic Association* 85, 607-608.
6. Alroomi, L.G., *et al.*: 1986, 'Maternal Narcotic Abuse and the Newborn', *Archives of Disease in Childhood* 63, 81-83.
7. American Academy of Pediatrics, Committee on Bioethics: 1988, 'Fetal Therapy: Ethical Considerations', *Pediatrics* 81, 898-899.
8. American Society of Anesthesiologists: 1974, 'Occupational Disease Among Operating Room Personnel: A National Study', *Anesthesiology* 41, 321-340.
9. Anderson, C.E.: 1989, 'When Faith Healing Fails', *ABA Journal*, July, 22-23.
10. Annas, G.J.: 1982, 'Forced Cesareans: The Most Unkindest Cut of All', *Hastings Center Report* 12, 16-18.
11. Annas, G.J.: 1986, 'Pregnant Women as Fetal Containers', *Hastings Center Report* 16, 13-14.
12. Aronson, M. and Olegard, R.: 1987, 'Children of Alcoholic Mothers', *Pediatrician* 14, 57-61.
13. Baker, M.L. and Dalrymple: 1984, 'Radiation and the Fetus', in W.R. Hendee (ed.), *Health Effects of Low-Level Radiation*, Appleton-Century-Croft, Norwalk, CT, pp. 127-130.
14. Ballantyne, B.: 1985, 'Evaluation of Hazards from Mixtures of Chemicals in the Occupational Environment', *Journal of Occupational Medicine* 27, 85-94.
15. Barnard, C.P.: 1984, 'Alcoholism and Incest', *Focus on Family and Chemical Dependency* 7, 27-29.
16. Bayer, R.: 1982, 'Women, Work, and Reproductive Hazards', *The Hastings Center Report* 12, 14-19.
17. Bayles, M.D.: 1984, *Reproductive Ethics*, Prentice-Hall, Inc., Englewood Cliffs, New Jersey.

18. Beal, R.: 1984 'Can I Sue Mommy? An Analysis of a Woman's Tort Liability for Prenatal Injuries to her Child Born Alive', *San Diego Law Review* 21, 325-370.
19. Beauchamp, T.L. and Childress, J. F.: 1983, *Principles of Biomedical Ethics*, 2nd Edition, Oxford University Press, New York.
20. Becker, L.C.: 1975, 'Human Being: The Boundaries of the Concept', *Philosophy and Public Affairs* 4, 334-359.
21. Behrman, R.E.: 1987, 'Premature Births Among Black Women', *New England Journal of Medicine* 312, 763-765.
22. Behrman, R.E.: 1985, 'Preventing Low Birthweight: A Pediatric Prospective', *Journal of Pediatrics* 107, 842-854.
23. Bertin, J.E.: 1989, 'Reproductive Hazards in the Workplace', in S. Cohen and N. Taub (eds), *Reproductive Laws for the 1990s*, Humana Press, Clifton, New Jersey.
24. Blanco, A.C.: 1985, 'Fetal Protection Programs Under Title VII–Rebutting the Procreation Presumption', *University of Pittsburgh Law Review* 46, 755-794.
25. Blank, R.: 1988, *Life, Death and Public Policy*, Northern Illinois University Press, DeKalb, Illinois.
26. Blume, S.B.: 1986, 'Is Social Drinking During Pregnancy Harmless? There is Reason to Think Not.' *Advances in Alcohol & Substance Abuse* 5, 209-219.
27. Blume, S.B.: 1987, 'Public Policy Issues Relevant to Children of Alcoholics', *Advances in Alcohol & Substance Abuse* 6, 5-15.
28. Borowski, T.A.: 1988, 'No Liability for the Wrongful Death of Unborn Children–the Florida Legislature Refuses to Protect the Unborn', *Florida State University Law Review* 16, 835-861.
29. Botkin, J.R.: 1988, 'The Legal Concept of Wrongful Life', *Journal of the American Medical Association* 259, 1541-1545.
30. Bowes, W.A. and Salgestad, B.: 1981, 'Fetal Versus Maternal Rights: Medical and Legal Perspectives', *Obstetrics and Gynecology* 58, 209-214.
31. Bureau of Labor Statistics, U.S. Department of Labor: 1988, *Employment and Earnings*, Government Printing Office, Washington, D.C.
32. Bush, M.: 1988, *Families in Distress*, University of California Press, Berkeley, CA.
33. Capron, A.M.: 1980, 'The Continuing Wrong of 'Wrongful Life',' in A. Milunsky and G.J. Annas (eds), *Genetics and the Law II*, Plenum Press, New York, pp. 81-93.
34. Carter, D.E. & Bellamy, W.T.: 1988, 'Toxicology of the Group III-V Intermediate Semiconductor, Gallium Arsenide', in T.W. Clarkson, *et. al.* (eds), *Biological Monitoring of Toxic Metals*, Plenum Press, New York, pp. 455-468.
35. Catz, C.S. and Yaffee, S.J.: 1976, 'Environmental Factors: Pharmacology', in National Institutes of Health, *Prevention of Embryonic, Fetal and Perinatal Disease*, Government Printing Office, Washington, D.C., pp. 119-145.
36. Chan, L.S. *et al.*: 1986, 'Differences Between Dropouts and Active Participants in a Pediatric Clinic for Substance Abuse Mothers', *American Journal of Drug and Alcohol Abuse* 12, 89-99.
37. Chasnoff, I.J.: 1989, 'Drug Use and Women: Establishing a Standard of Care', in Donald E. Hutchings (ed.), *Prenatal Abuse of Licit and Illicit Drugs*, The New York Academy of Medicine, New York, pp. 208-210.
38. Chasnoff, I.J., *et al.*: 1986, 'Prenatal Drug Exposure: Effects on Neonatal & Infant Growth & Development', *Neurobehavioral Toxicology and Teratology* 8, 357-362.

39. Chasnoff, I.J.: 1987, 'Perinatal Effects of Cocaine', *Contemporary Obstetrics and Gynecology* 29, 163-179.
40. Chasnoff, I.J., *et al.*: 1990, 'The Prevalence of Illicit-drug or Alcohol Use During Pregnancy and Discrepancies in Mandatory Reporting in Pinellas County, Florida', *New England Journal of Medicine* 322, 1202-1206.
41. Childress, J.F.: 1982, *Who Should Decide? Paternalism in Health Care*, Oxford University Press, New York.
42. Churchville, V.: 1988, 'D.C. Judge Jails Woman as Protection for Fetus', *Washington Post*, July 23, A1 and 8.
43. Clarkson, T.W. *et. al.*, (eds): 1988, *Biological Monitoring of Toxic Metals*, Plenum Press, New York.
44. Clarkson, T.W., *et al.*(eds): 1983, *Reproductive and Developmental Toxicity of Metals*, Plenum Press, New York.
45. Clarren, S.K. and Smith, D.W.: 1978, 'The Fetal Alcohol Syndrome,' *New England Journal of Medicine* 298, 1063-1067.
46. Cnattingius, S., *et al.*: 1985, 'Smoking, Maternal Age, and Fetal Growth', *Obstetrics and Gynecology* 66, 449-452.
47. 'Cocaine Babies: The Littlest Victims:' 1989, *Newsweek*, November 13, 55.
48. Cohen, E.N., *et al.*: 1971, 'Anesthesia, Pregnancy, and Miscarriage: A Study of Operating Room Nurses and Anesthetists', *Anesthesiology* 34, 343-347.
49. Cole, C.D., *et al.*: 1984, 'Neonatal Ethanol Withdrawal: Characteristics in Clinically Normal, Nondysmorphic Neonates', *Journal of Pediatrics* 105, 445-471.
50. Collins, J.J. and Allison, M.: 1983, 'Legal Coercion and Retention in Drug Abuse Treatment', *Hospital and Community Psychiatry* 34, 1145-1149.
51. 'Comment: Criminal Liability of a Prospective Mother for Prenatal Neglect of a Viable Fetus:' 1987, *Whittier Law Review* 9, 363-396.
52. 'Comment: Tort Actions Between Members of the Family–Husband and Wife, Parent and Child:' 1961, *Missouri Law Review* 26, 152-174.
53. Committee on Ethics: 1987, 'Statement of the Committee on Ethics', American College of Obstetricians and Gynecologists, Washington, D.C.
54. Committee on Nutrition: 1974, *Nutrition in Maternal Health Care*, American College of Obstetricians and Gynecologists, Chicago.
55. Committee on Ways and Means, U.S. House of Representatives: 1985, *Children in Poverty*, Government Printing Office, Washington, D.C.
56. Committee to Study the Prevention of Low Birthweight, Institute of Medicine: 1985, *Preventing Low Birthweight*, National Academy Press, Washington, D.C.
57. Cook, W.: 1970, 'Incompetent Donors: Was the First Step or the Last Taken in Strunk v. Strunk?' *California Law Review* 58, 754-774.
58. Costin, L.B. and Rapp, C.A.: 1984, *Child Welfare: Policies and Practice, 3rd edition*, McGraw-Hill, New York.
59. Cotton, D.: 1983, 'Abnormal Labor and Delivery', in K.R. Niswander (ed.), *Manual of Obstetrics*, 2nd ed., Little, Brown and Co., Boston, pp. 357-384.
60. Council on Scientific Affairs, American Medical Association: 1983, 'Fetal Effects of Maternal Alcohol Use', *Journal of the American Medical Association* 249, 2517-2521.
61. Curriden, M.: 1990, 'Holding Mom Accountable', *ABA Journal*, March, 51-53.
62. 'Danger on the Job:' 1989, *Newsweek*, December 11, 42-46.

63. D'Arcy, E.: 1963, *Human Acts: An Essay in Their Moral Evaluation*, Clarendon Press, Oxford.
64. Department of Health, Education and Welfare: 1979, *Smoking and Health: A Report of the Surgeon General*, Government Printing Office, Washington, D.C.
65. Deren, S.: 1986, 'The Children of Substance Abusers: A Review of the Literature', *Journal of Substance Abuse Treatment* 3, 77-94.
66. 'Developments in the Law: The Constitution and the Family', 1980, *Harvard Law Review* 93, 1156-1383.
67. 'Disease the Focus of Programs to Reduce Infant Mortality:' 1988, *Infectious Diseases in Children*, 20.
68. Doberczak, T.M., *et al.*: 1988, 'Neonatal Neurologic & Electroencephalographic Effects of Intrauterine Cocaine Exposure', *Journal of Pediatrics* 113, 354-358.
69. Dutton, D.B.: 1988, *Worse than the Disease: Pitfalls of Medical Progress*, Cambridge University Press, New York.
70. Dworkin, R.: 1977, *Taking Rights Seriously*, Harvard University Press, Cambridge, MA.
71. Dworkin, R.: 1979, 'We Do Not Have a Right to Liberty,' in R. Cunningham (ed.), *Liberty and the Rule of Law*, Texas A & M University Press, College Station, Texas.
72. Edelin, K.C. *et al.*: 1988, 'Methadone Maintenance in Pregnancy: Consequences to Care and Outcome', *Obstetrics and Gynecology*, 7, 399-404.
73. Ehrenkranz, S.M., *et al.* (eds): 1989, *Clinical Social Work with Maltreated Children and Their Families*, New York University Press, New York.
74. Elias, S. and Annas, G.J. (eds): 1987, *Reproductive Genetics and the Law*, Chicago Year Book, Chicago.
75. Engelhardt, H.T.: 1985, 'Current Controversies in Obstetrics: Wrongful Life and Forced Fetal Surgical Procedures', *American Journal of Obstetrics and Gynecology* 151, 313-318.
76. Enthovan, A. and Kronick, R.: 1989, 'A Consumer-Choice Health Plan for the 1990s', *New England Journal of Medicine* 320, 29-37.
77. Evans, R.W., *et al.*: 1984, *The National Heart Transplantation Study: Final Report*, Battelle Human Affairs Research Centers, Seattle.
78. Faden, R.R. and Beauchamp, T.L.: 1986, *A History and Theory of Informed Consent*, Oxford University Press, New York.
79. Fadiman, A.: 1983, 'The Unborn Patient', *Life* 6, 38-44.
80. Feinberg, J.: 1970, 'The Expressive Function of Punishment', in *Doing and Deserving*, Princeton University Press, Princeton, New Jersey, pp. 95-118.
81. Feinberg, J.: 1980, 'Is There a Right to be Born?' *Rights, Justice, and the Bounds of Liberty*, Princeton University Press, Princeton, N.J., pp. 207-220.
82. Feinberg, J.: 1984, *The Moral Limits of the Criminal Law, Volume One, Harm to Others*, Oxford University Press, New York.
83. Feinberg, J.: 1984, *The Problem of Abortion*, 2nd ed., Wadsworth, Belmont, CA.
84. Feinberg, J.: 1986, 'Abortion', in Tom Regan (ed.) *Matters of Life and Death* 2nd ed., Random House, New York, pp. 257-293.
85. Feinberg, J.: 1986, 'Wrongful Life and the Counterfactual Element in Harming', *Social Philosophy and Policy* 4, 145-178.
86. Field, M.A.: 1989, 'Controlling the Woman to Protect the Fetus', *Law, Medicine and*

Health Care 17, 114-129.

87. Finnegan, L.P.: 1982, 'Outcome of Children Born to Women Dependent upon Narcotics', *Advances in Alcohol and Substance Abuse*, 55-101.
88. Fisher, E.S., *et al.*: 1985, 'Prenatal Care and Pregnancy Outcomes During the Recession: The Washington State Experience', *American Journal of Public Health* 75, 866-869.
89. Fitzsimmons, J., *et al.*: 1986, 'Pregnancy in a Drug-abusing Population', *American Journal of Drug & Alcohol Abuse* 12, 247-55.
90. Flandermeyer, A.A.: 1987, 'A Comparison of the Effects of Heroin and Cocaine Abuse upon the Neonate', *Neonatal Network*, December, 42-48.
91. Fleisher, L.D.P: 1987, 'Wrongful Births: When Is There Liability for Prenatal Injury?' *American Journal of the Diseases of Children* 141, 1260-1265.
92. Fletcher, J.: 1981, 'The Fetus as Patient: Ethical Issues', *Journal of the American Medical Association* 246, 772-773.
93. Fletcher, J.: 1986, 'Drawing Moral Lines in Fetal Therapy', *Clinical Obstetrics and Gynecology* 29, 595-602.
94. Footlick, J.K.: 1990, 'What Happened to the Family?' *Newsweek*, Winter/Spring, 15-20.
95. Fost, N., *et al.*: 1980, 'The Limited Moral Significance of 'Fetal Viability',' *Hastings Center Report* 10, 10-13.
96. Frank, D.A., *et al.*: 1988, 'Cocaine Use During Pregnancy: Prevalence and Correlates', *Pediatrics* 82, 888-895.
97. Freudenheim, M.: 1989, 'Company Programs to Avoid 'Preemies', *New York Times*, December 28, C1, 3.
98. Gallagher, J.: 1985, 'Fetal Personhood and Women's Policy', in V. Shapiro (ed.) *Sage Yearbooks in Women's Policy Studies*, Sage Publications, Beverly Hills, CA., 91-116.
99. Gallagher, J.: 1989, 'Position Paper: Fetus as Patient', in S. Cohen & N. Taub (eds), *Reproductive Laws for the 1990s*, Humana Press, Clifton, New Jersey, pp. 185-236.
100. Gini, A.R. and Sullivan, T.J.: 1989, *It Comes with the Territory: An Inquiry Concerning Work and the Person*, Random House, New York.
101. Glantz, L.H.: 1976, 'The Legal Aspects of Fetal Viability', in A. Milunsky and G.J. Annas (eds), *Genetics and the Law*, Plenum Press, New York, pp. 29-43.
102. Glass, L. and Evans, H.E.: 1979, 'Perinatal Drug Abuse', *Pediatric Annals* 8, 41-62.
103. Gleicher, N.: 1984, 'Cesarean Section Rates in the United States', *Journal of the American Medical Association* 252, 3273-3276.
104. Goldstein, J.: 1982, 'Medical Care for the Child at Risk: On State Supervision of Parental Autonomy', in W. Gaylin and R. Macklin (eds), *Who Speaks for the Child? The Problem of Proxy Consent*, Plenum Press, New York, pp. 153-188.
105. Gortmaker, S.L.: 1979, 'The Effects of Prenatal Care Upon the Health of the Newborn', *American Journal of Public Health* 69, 653-660.
106. Hanson, J.W., *et al.*: 1978, 'The Effects of Moderate Alcohol Consumption During Pregnancy on Fetal Growth and Morphogenesis', *Journal of Pediatrics* 93: 457-460.
107. Harrison, M.R.: 1982, 'Unborn: Historical Perspective of the Fetus as Patient', *The Pharos* 45, 19-24.
108. Harrison, M.R., *et al.*: 1982, 'Fetal Treatment 1982', *The New England Journal of Medicine* 307, 1651-1652.

109. Hart, H.L.A.: 1976, *Punishment and Responsibility*, Oxford University Press, New York.
110. Henig, R.M.: 1982, 'Saving Babies Before Birth', *New York Times Magazine*, February 28.
111. Hill, R.M. and Desmond, M.M.: 1963, 'Management of the Narcotic Withdrawal Syndrome in the Neonate', *Pediatric Clinicians of North America* 10, 67-85.
112. Hill, R.M., *et al.*: 1977, 'Utilization of Over-the-Counter Drugs During Pregnancy', *Clinical Obstetrics and Gynecology* 20, 381-394.
113. Himaka, M.: 1987, 'Judge Drops Prenatal Care Case Against Mother', *The San Diego Union*, February 27, A1.
114. Himmelstein, D.U., *et al.*: 1989, 'A National Health Program for the United States: A Physicians' Proposal', *New England Journal of Medicine* 320, 102-108.
115. Honoré, A.M.: 1966, 'Law, Morals, and Rescue', in J.M. Ratcliffe (ed.), *The Good Samaritan and the Law*, Doubleday and Co., Inc., New York, pp. 225-242.
116. International Surgery Registry: 1986, 'Catheter Shunts for Fetal Hydronephrosis and Hydrocephalus', *New England Journal of Medicine* 315, 336-340.
117. Isozol, J.: 1990, 'The New Untouchables', *Newsweek*, Winter/Spring, 48-53.
118. Johnsen, D.: 1986, 'The Creation of Fetal Rights: Conflicts with Women's Constitutional Rights to Liberty, Privacy, and Equal Protection', *Yale Law Journal* 95, 599-625.
119. Johnsen, D.: 1987, 'A New Threat to Pregnant Women's Autonomy', *Hastings Center Report* 17, 33-40.
120. Joyce, K., *et al.*: 1983, 'Internal and External Barriers to Obtaining Prenatal Care', *Social Work and Health Care* 9, 89-96.
121. Jurow, R. and Paul, R.H.: 1984, 'Cesarean Delivery for Fetal Distress Without Maternal Consent', *Obstetrics and Gynecology* 63, 596-598.
122. Kempe, C.H. and Helfer, R., (eds): 1980, *The Battered Child*, University of Chicago Press, Chicago.
123. Kirsch-Volders, M. (ed.): 1984, *Mutagenicity, Carcinogenicity and Teratogenicity of Industrial Pollutants*, Plenum Press, New York.
124. Knill-Jones, R.P., *et al.*: 1972, 'Anesthetic Practice and Pregnancy: Controlled Study of Women Anesthetists in the United Kingdon', *Lancet* 1, 1326-1328.
125. Kolder, V.E.B., *et al.*: 1987, 'Court-Ordered Obstetrical Interventions', *The New England Journal of Medicine* 316, 1192-1196.
126. Kosten, T.R., *et al.*: 1986, 'Cocaine Abuse Among Opiod Addicts: Demographic and Diagnostic Factors in Treatment', *American Journal of Drug and Alcohol Abuse* 12, 1-16.
127. Kreek, M.: 1982, 'Ophiod Disposition and Effects During Chronic Exposure in the Perinatal Period in Man', *Advances in Alcohol & Substance Abuse* 34, 21-53.
128. Kushner, H.I.: 1989, *Self-Destruction in the Promised Land: A Psychocultural History*, Rutgers University Press, New Jersey.
129. Laird, J. and Hartman, A., (eds): 1985, *A Handbook of Child Welfare*, The Free Press, New York.
130. Lappé, M.: 1975, 'The Moral Claims of the Wanted Fetus', *The Hastings Center Report* 5, 11-13.
131. Leu, L.: 1986, 'Legislative Research Bureau Report: A Proposal to Strengthen State

Measures for the Reduction of Infant Mortality', *Harvard Journal of Legislation* 23, 559-578.
132. Levmore, S.: 1986, 'Waiting for Rescue: An Essay on the Evolution and Incentive Structure of the Law of Affirmative Obligations', *Virginia Law Review* 72, 879-941.
133. Lewin, T.: 1987, 'Courts Acting to Force Care of the Unborn', *New York Times*, November 23, A1.
134. Little, R.E.: 1977, 'Moderate Alcohol Use During Pregnancy and Decreased Infant Birth Weight', *American Journal of Public Health* 67, 1154-1156.
135. Little, R.E., *et al.*: 1982, 'Fetal Alcohol Effects in Humans and Animals', *Advances in Alcohol & Substance Abuse*, 103-125.
136. Little, R.E. and Sing, C.F.: 1987, 'Father's Drinking and Infant Birthweight: Report of an Association', *Teratology* 36, 59-65.
137. LoBue, C.C.: 1983, 'Effects of Drugs on the Fetus', in Kenneth R. Niswander (ed.), *Manual of Obstetrics*, Little, Brown, Boston, pp. 281-304.
138. Lomansky, L.E.: 1987, *Persons, Rights, and the Moral Community*, Oxford University Press, New York.
139. Longo, L.M.: 1982, 'Health Consequences of Maternal Smoking', in the National Research Council, *Alternative Dietary Practices and Nutritional Abuses in Pregnancy*, National Academy Press, Washington, D.C.
140. Luker, K.: 1984, *Abortion and the Politics of Motherhood*, University of California Press, Berkeley.
141. Mackenzie, T.M. and Nagel, T.C.: 1986, 'Commentary: When a Pregnant Woman Endangers Her Fetus', *Hastings Center Report* 16, 24-25.
142. MacGregnor, S.N., *et al.*: 1987, 'Cocaine Use During Pregnancy: Adverse Perinatal Outcome', *American Journal of Obstetrics and Gynecology* 1587, 686-689.
143. Macklin, R.: 1988, 'The Inner Workings of an Ethics Committee: Latest Battle over Jehovah's Witnesses', *Hastings Center Report* 18, 15-20.
144. Madden, J.D., *et al.*: 1986, 'Maternal Cocaine Abuse and Effect on the Newborn', *Pediatrics* 77, 209-211.
145. Mahowald, M.: 1989, 'Beyond Abortion: Refusal of Cesarean Section', *Bioethics* 3, 106-121.
146. Marcotte, P.: 1989, 'Crime and Pregnancy', *ABA Journal*, August, 14-15.
147. Marcus, J., Hans, S., and Jeremy, R.J.: 1984, 'A Longitudinal Study of Offspring Born to Methadone-maintained Women. III. Effects of Multiple Risk Factors on Development at 4, 8, and 12 Months', *American Journal of Drug and Alcohol Abuse* 10, 195-207.
148. Mark, F.: 1988, 'Does Coercion Work? The Role of Referral Source in Motivating Alcoholics in Treatment', *Alcoholism Treatment Quarterly* 5, 5-22.
149. Marx, K.: 1977, *Capital: A Critique of Political Economy* (1859), D. Fernbach (trans.). Vintage Books, New York.
150. Mathieu, D.: 1985, 'Respecting Liberty and Preventing Harm: Limits of State Intervention in Prenatal Choice', *Harvard Journal of Law & Public Policy* 8, 19-55.
151. McCormick, M.C.: 1985, 'The Contribution of Low Birth Weight to Infant Mortality and Childhood Morbidity', *New England Journal of Medicine* 312, 82-90.
152. McElveen, J.C.: 1985, 'Reproductive Hazards in the Workplace', *The Forum* 20, 547-571.

153. Medicare Catastrophic Illness Protection Act: 1988, Section 302, Public Law 100-360.
154. Merkatz, I.R., *et al.*: 1980, 'Ritodrine Hydrochloride: A Betamimetic Agent for Use in Preterm Labor. II. Evidence of Efficacy', *Obstetrics and Gynecology* 56, 7-13.
155. Mills, J.L., *et al.*: 1984, 'Maternal Alcohol Consumption and Birth Weight', *Journal of the American Medical Association* 252, 1875-1879.
156. Missouri Revised Statute 1.205.1: 1986.
157. Mitchell, J.B. and Cromwell, J.: 1980, 'Medicaid Mills: Fact or Fiction?', *Health Care Financing Review* 1, 37-49.
158. Moore, T.R., *et al.*: 1986, 'The Perinatal and Economic Impact of Prenatal Care in a Low-Socioeconomic Population', *American Journal of Obstetrics and Gynecology* 154, 29-33.
159. Morreim, E.H.: 1988, 'The Concept of Harm Reconceived: A Different Look at Wrongful Life', *Law and Philosophy* 7, 3-33.
160. Murray, J.L. and Bernfield, M.: 1988, 'The Differential Effect of Prenatal Care on the Incidence of Low Birth Weight Among Blacks and Whites in a Prepaid Health Plan', *New England Journal of Medicine* 319, 1385-1391.
161. Murray, T.M.: 1985, 'Who Do Fetal-Protection Policies Really Protect?' *Technology Review* 88, 12-13, 20.
162. Nadel, M.: 1985, 'Offspring with Fetal Alcohol Effects', in D. Cook, *et al.* (eds), *Psychosocoial Issues in the Treatment of Alcoholism*, Haworth Press, New York.
163. Naeye, R.L., *et al.*: 1973, 'Effects of Maternal Nutrition on the Human Fetus', *Pediatrics* 52, 494-500.
164. National Center on Child Abuse and Neglect, U.S. Children's Bureau, U.S. Department of Health and Human Services: 1978, *Substance Abuse and Child Abuse and Neglect*, Government Printing Office, Washington, D.C.
165. 'National Health Plan Wins Unlikely Backer: Business:' 1989, *Wall Street Journal*, April 5.
166. 'National Institutes of Health, Consensus Development Task Force Statement on Cesarean Childbirth:' 1981, *American Journal of Obstetrics and Gynecology* 39, 902-909.
167. Nazario, S.L.: 1988, 'High Infant Mortality Is a Persistent Blotch On Health Care in U.S.', *Wall Street Journal*, October 19.
168. Nelson, L.J. and Milliken, N.: 1988, 'Compelled Medical Treatment of Pregnant Women: Life, Liberty and Law in Conflict', *Journal of the American Medical Association* 259, 1060-1066.
169. Norton, F.C., *et al.*: 1987, 'Comparisons of National Cesarean-Section Rates', *New England Journal of Medicine* 316, 386-390.
170. Note: 1985, 'Faith Healing Exemptions to Child Protection Laws: Keeping the Faith Versus Medical Care for Children', *Journal of Legislation* 12, 243-263.
171. Note: 1978, 'Parental Liability for Prenatal Injuries: The Right of a Child Against its Mother', *Suffolk University Law Review* 10, 582-603.
172. Office of Technology Assessment: 1985, *Reproductive Health Hazards in the Workplace: Summary*, Government Printing Office, Washington, D.C.
173. Olson, J., *et al.*: 1983, 'Alcohol Use, Conception Time and Birthweight', *Journal of Epidemiology and Community Health* 37, 63-75.
174. Omnibus Budget Reconciliation Act: 1987, Section 4101, Public Law 100-203.

175. Oro, A.S., Dixon, S.D.: 1987, 'Perinatal Cocaine and Metamphetamine Exposure: Maternal and Neonatal Correlates', *Journal of Pediatrics* 222, 571-578.
176. Orstead, C., *et al.*: 1985, 'Efficacy of Prenatal Nutrition Counseling: Weight Gain, Infant Birth Weight, and Cost-Effectiveness', *Journal of the American Dietic Association* 85, 40-45.
177. Parness, J.: 1985, 'Crimes Against the Unborn', *Harvard Journal on Legislation* 22, 97-172.
178. Phillips, C. and Johnson, N.: 1977, 'The Impact of Quality of Diet and Other Factors on Birth Weight of Infants', *American Journal of Clinical Nutrition* 30, 215-221.
179. Plant, M.L. and Plant, M.A.: 1987, 'Family Alcohol Problems Among Pregnant Women: Links with Maternal Substance Use and Birth Abnormalities', *Drug & Alcohol Dependence* 20, 213-219.
180. Poland, M.L., *et al.*: 1987, 'Barriers to Receiving Adequate Prenatal Care', *American Journal of Obstetrics and Gynecology* 157, 297-303.
181. 'Pregnant Teen Held for Safety of Fetus',: 1985, *St. Paul Pioneer Press and Dispatch*, August 16, A3.
182. Prentice, R.A.: 1985: 'Expanding the Duty to Rescue,' *Suffolk University Law Review* 19, 15-54.
183. President's Commission for the Study of Ethical Problems in Medicine and Biomedical and Behavioral Research: 1983, *Securing Access to Health Care, Volume One: Report*, Government Printing Office, Washington, D.C.
184. Rahbar, F., *et al.*: 1985, 'Prenatal Care and Perinatal Mortality in a Black Population', *Obstetrics and Gynecology* 65, 327-329.
185. Relman, A.S.: 1989, 'Universal Health Insurance: Its Time Has Come', *New England Journal of Medicine* 320, 117-118.
186. Retshesky, R.: 1979, 'Workers, Reproductive Hazards, & the Politics of Protection: An Introduction', *Feminist Studies* 5, 233-246.
187. Rhoden, N.K.: 1986, 'Judges in the Delivery Room', *California Law Review* 74, 1951-2030.
188. Rhoden, N.K.: 1987, 'Cesareans and Samaritans', *Law, Medicine and Health Care* 15, 118-125.
189. Robertson, J.A.: 1976, 'Organ Donations by Incompetents and the Substituted Judgment Doctrine', *Columbia Law Review* 76, 48-78.
190. Robertson, J.A.: 1982, 'The Right to Procreate and *in Utero* Fetal Therapy', *Journal of Legal Medicine* 3, 333-366.
191. Robertson, J.A.: 1983, 'Procreative Liberty and the Control of Conception, Pregnancy, and Childbirth', *Virginia Law Review* 69, 405-464.
192. Robitaille, Y. and Kramer, M.S.: 1985, 'Does Participation in Prenatal Courses Lead to Heavier Babies?' *American Journal of Public Health* 75, 1186-1189.
193. Rodgers, H.R.: 1986, *Poor Women, Poor Families*, M.E. Sharpe, Inc., Armonk, New York.
194. Rosenbaum, S. and Johnson, K.: 1986, 'Providing Health Care for Low-income Children: Reconciling Child Health Goals with Child Health Financing Realities', *The Milbank Quarterly* 64, 442-478.
195. Rosenbaum, S., *et al.*: 1988, 'Incantations in the Dark: Medicaid, Managed Care, and Maternity Care', *Milbank Quarterly* 4, 661-693.

196. Rosso, R.: 1981, 'Nutrition and Maternal-Fetal Exchange', *American Journal of Clinical Nutrition* 34, 744-781.
197. Rothenberg, K.: 1988, 'Medical Decision Making for Children', in J.F. Childress *et al.* (eds), *BioLaw, Volume I*, University Publications of America, Frederick, Maryland, pp. 149-176.
198. Rothman, B.K.: 1986, 'When a Pregnant Woman Endangers Her Fetus: Commentary', *Hastings Center Report* 16, 25.
199. Roy, D.J.: 1988, 'Fetal Therapy: Ethical Considerations', in C. Nimrod and G. Griener (eds), *Biomedical Ethics and Fetal Therapy*, Wilfrid Laurier University Press, Ontario, Canada, pp. 59-66.
200. Rubin, D.H., *et al.*: 1988, 'Cigarette Smoking and Alcohol Consumption During Pregnancy by Danish Women and Their Spouses: A Potential Source of Fetal Morbidity', *American Journal of Drug and Alcohol Abuse* 14, 405-417.
201. Rush, D., *et al.*: 1988, 'The National WIC Evaluation: Evaluation of the Special Supplemental Food Program for Women, Infants, and Children, III, Historical Study of Pregnancy Outcomes', *American Journal of Clinical Nutrition* 48, 412-428.
202. Sager, P.R., *et al.*: 1986, 'Reproductive and Developmental Toxicity of Metals', in L. Friberg, *et al.* (eds), *Handbook on the Toxicology of Metals, Volume II*, Elsevier, New York.
203. Samborn, R.: 1989, 'Seventh Circuit Bias Ruling Criticized', *National Law Journal*, October 16, 1-30.
204. Savitz, D., *et al.*: 1989, 'Effect of Parents' Occupational Exposures on Risk of Stillbirth, Preterm Delivery, and Small-for-gestational-age Infants', *American Journal of Epidemiology* 129, 1201-1218.
205. Schachter, J.: 1986, 'Help is Hard to Find for Addict Mothers: Drug Use 'Epidemic' Overwhelms Services', *Los Angeles Times*, December 12, II-1.
206. Schramm, W.F.: 1985, 'WIC Prenatal Participation and Its Relationship to Newborn Medical Costs in Missouri: A Cost/Benefit Analysis', *American Journal of Public Health* 75, 851-857.
207. Shaw, M.W.: 1984, 'Conditional Prospective Rights of the Fetus', *The Journal of Legal Medicine* 5, 63-116.
208. Shaw, M.W.: 1977, 'Genetically Defective Children: Emerging Legal Considerations', *American Journal of Law & Medicine* 3, 333-340.
209. Shaw, M.W.: 1980, 'The Potential Plaintiff: Preconception & Prenatal Torts', in A. Milunsky and A.J. Annas (eds) *Genetics and the Law II*, Plenum Press, New York.
210. Shaw, M.W. and Doudera, A.E. (eds): 1983, *Defining Human Life: Medical, Legal & Ethical Implications*, AUPHA press, Ann Arbor, Michigan.
211. Sherman, R.: 1989, 'Keeping Babies Free of Drugs', *The National Law Journal*, October 16, 1, 28-29.
212. Sherman, R.: 1988, 'Keeping Baby Safe From Mom', *The National Law Journal*, October 3, 1, 24-25.
213. Shiono, P.H., *et al.*: 1986, 'Smoking and Drinking During Pregnancy', *Journal of the American Medical Association* 255, 82-84.
214. Sidel, R.: 1986, *Women and Children Last*, Penguin Books, New York.
215. Simon, C.: 1978, 'Parental Liability for Prenatal Injury', *Columbia Journal of Law and Social Problems* 14, 47-92.

216. Singer, P.A., *et al.*: 1989, 'Ethics of Liver Transportation with Living Donors', *New England Journal of Medicine* 321, 620-622.
217. Smith, H.M.: 1983, 'Intercourse and Moral Responsibility for the Fetus', in W. B. Bondesson (ed.), *Abortion and the Status of the Fetus*, D. Reidel Publishing Co., Holland, 229-245.
218. Sokol, R.J. *et al.*: 1980, 'Alcohol Abuse During Pregnancy: An Epidemiological Study.' *Alcoholism: Clinical and Experimental Research* 4, 135-145.
219. Starfield, B.: 1985, 'Motherhood and Apple Pie: The Effectiveness of Medical Care for Children', *Milbank Memorial Fund Quarterly* 63, 523-546.
220. Starozewski, M.: 1986, 'Wrongful Death of a Fetus: Does a Cause of Action Arise When There is No Live Birth?' *Villanova Law Review* 31, 659-695.
221. Stein, Z., and Kline, J: 1983, 'Editorial: Smoking, Alcohol and Reproduction', *American Journal of Public Health* 73, 1154-1156.
222. Steinbock, B.: 1986, 'The Logical Case for Wrongful Life', *Hastings Center Report* 16, 15-20.
223. Strobino, B.R., *et al.*: 1978, 'Chemical and Physical Exposures of Parents: Effects on Human Reproduction and Offspring', *Early Human Development* 1, 371-399.
224. Sumner, L.W.: 1987, *The Moral Foundation of Rights*, Oxford University Press, New York.
225. Taffer, S., *et al.*: 1987, 'Trends in the United States Cesarian Section Rate and Reasons for the 1980-85 Rise', *American Journal of Public Health* 77, 955-959.
226. Tannenbaum, T. and Goldberg, R.J.: 1985, 'Exposure to Anesthetic Gases and Reproductive Outcome–A Review of the Epidemiologic Literature', *Journal of Occupational Medicine* 27, 659-668.
227. Task Force on Organ Transplantation: 1986, *Organ Transplantation: Issues and Recommendations*, Government Printing Office, Washington, D.C.
228. Thomson, J.J.: 1971, 'A Defense of Abortion', *Philosophy and Public Affairs* 1, 47-66.
229. Trost, C.: 1989, 'Born to Lose', *Wall Street Journal*, July 18.
230. Veatch, R.: 1984, 'Limits of Guardian Treatment Refusal: A Reasonableness Standard', *American Journal of Law and Medicine* 9, 427-470.
231. Wallis, C.: 1989, 'Onward, Women!' *Time*, December 4, 80-89.
232. Warren, M.A.: 1973, 'On the Moral and Legal Status of the Fetus', *The Monist* 57, 43-61.
233. Waterson, J. and Ettorre, B.: 1989, 'Providing Services for Women with Difficulties with Alcohol or Other Drugs: The Current U.K. Situation as Seen by Women Practioners, Researchers, and Policy Makers in the Field', *Drug and Alcohol Dependence* 24, 119-125.
234. Weinrib, E.J.: 1980, 'The Case for a Duty to Rescue', *Yale Law Journal* 90, 247-293.
235. Wellman, C.: 1985, *A Theory of Rights*, Roman and Allanheld, Totowa, New Jersey.
236. Westermeyer, J.: 1989, 'Nontreatment Factors Affecting Treatment Outcomes in Substance Abuse', *American Journal of Drug & Alcohol Abuse* 15, 13-29.
237. 'When the Courts Take Charge of the Unborn': 1983, *New York Times*, April 27, A-18.
238. Williams, W.W.: 1981, 'Firing the Woman to Protect the Fetus: The Reconciliation of Fetal Protection with Employment Opportunity Goals Under Title VII', *The*

Georgetown Law Review 69, 641-704.

239. Wilson, G.S.: 1989, 'Clinical Studies of Infants and Children Exposed Prenatally to Heroin', in D. E. Hutchings (ed.), *Prenatal Abuse of Licit and Illicit Drugs*, The New York Academy of Medicine, New York, pp. 183-194.
240. Wilson, G.S., Desmond, M.M., and Wait, R.B.: 1981, 'Follow-up of Methadone-treated and Untreated Narcotic-dependent Women and Their Infants: Health, Developmental, and Social Implications', *Journal of Pediatrics* 98, 716-722.
241. Wilson, P.A., *et al.*: 1988, 'Providing Medical Care for the Poor: Medicaid in a Period of Transition', in E.M. Melhado, *et al.* (eds), *Money, Power and Health Care*, Health Administration Press, Ann Arbor, pp. 183-208.
242. Zuckerman, B., *et al.*: 1989, 'Effects of Maternal Marijauna and Cocaine Use on Fetal Growth', *New England Journal of Medicine* 320, 762-8.

Legal Cases

243. *Albala v. City of New York*: 1981, 434 N.Y.S.2d 400.
244. *Application of the President and Directors of Georgetown College Inc.*: 1964, 331 F.2d 1000 (D.C. Cir.), *cert. denied* 337 U.S. 978.
245. *Beal v. Doe*: 1977, 432 U.S. 438.
246. *Becker v. Schwartz*: 1978, 46 N.Y.2d 401, 386 N.E.2d 807, 413 N.Y.S.2d 895.
247. *Bellis v. U.S.*: 1974, 417 U.S. 85.
248. *Bergstresser v. Mitchell*: 1978, 577 F.2d 22.
249. *Bowden v. State*: 1974, 256 Ark. 820, 510 S.W.2d 879.
250. *Breithaupt v. Abram*: 1957, 352 U.S. 432.
251. *Buck v. Bell*: 1927, 274 U.S. 200.
252. *City of Akron v. Center for Reproductive Health*: 1983, 462 U.S. 416.
253. *Colautti v. Franklin*: 1979, 439 U.S. 379.
254. *Commonwealth v. Daniel I. Cass*: 1984, 392 Mass. 799, 467 N.E. Rptr. 1324.
255. *Curlender v. Bio-Science Laboratories*: 1980, 106 Cal. App. 3d 811, 165 Cal. Rptr. 477.
256. *Dennis v. Walker*: 1968, 284 F. Supp. 413.
257. *Farwell v. Keaton*: 1976, 396 Mich. 281, 240 N.W.2d 217.
258. *First National Bank v. Bellotti*: 1978, 435 U.S. 765.
259. *Gibson v. Gibson*: 1971, 3 Cal.3d 914, 479 P.2d 648, 92 Cal. Rptr. 288.
260. *Goldberg v. Ruskin*: 1986, 499 N.E.2d 406.
261. *Goller v. White*: 1963, 20 Wis.2d 402, 122 N.W.2d 193.
262. *Grayned v. City of Rockford*: 1971, 408 U.S. 104.
263. *Griswold v. Connecticut*: 1965, 381 U.S. 479.
264. *Harris v. McRae*: 1980, 448 U.S. 297.
265. *Hastings v. Hastings*: 1960, 33 N.J. 247, 163 A.2d 147.
266. *Hayes v. Shelby Memorial Hospital*: 1984, 726 F.2d 1543 (11th. Cir.).
267. *In re Baby X*: 1980, 97 Mich. App. 111, 293 N.W.2d 736.
268. *In re Infant Doe*: 1982, No. GU 8204-004A (Monroe County Circuit Court).
269. *In re Philip B.*: 1980, 92 Cal. App. 3d 796, *cert. denied* 445 U.S. 949.
270. *In re Ruiz*, 1986, 500 N.E.2d 935.
271. *In re Steven S.*: 1981, 126 Cal. App.3d 23, 178 Cal. Rptr. 525.
272. *International Union, United Automobile, Aerospace and Agricultural Implement Workers of America, et al. v. Johnson Controls, Inc.*: 1989, 886 F.2d 871 (7th Cir.).
273. *Jacobsen v. Massachusetts*: 1905, 197 U.S. 11.

274. *Jefferson v. Griffin Spalding County Hospital Authority*: 1981, 247 Ga. 86, 274 S.E.2d 457
275. *Jorgensen v. Meade Johnson Laboratories, Inc.*: 1973, 483 F.2d 237.
276. *Keeler v. Superior Court of Amador County*: 1970, 2 Cal.3d 619, 87 Cal. Rptr. 481, 470 P.2d 617.
277. *Little v. Little*: 1979, 576 S.E.2d 493.
278. *Loving v. Virginia*: 1967, 388 U.S. 1.
279. *Maher v. Roe*: 1977, 432 U.S. 464.
280. *McFall v. Shimp*: 1978, No. 78-17711 In Equity (C.P. Allegheny County, PA).
281. *NAACP v. Button*: 1963, 371 U.S. 415.
282. *Natanson v. Kline*: 1960, 186 Kan. 393, 350 P.2d 670.
283. *Park v. Chessin*: 1977, 400 N.Y.S. 110.
284. *People v. Stewart*: 1987, No. M508197 (San Diego Municipal Court), Miller, E.L., Jr. and Phillips, R.C.: 'Points and Authorities in Opposition to Defendant's Demurrer and Motion to Dismiss.'
285. *Pierce v. Society of Sisters*: 1925, 268 U.S. 510.
286. *Planned Parenthood of Central Missouri v. Danforth*: 1976, 438 U.S. 52.
287. *Presley v. Newport Hospital*: 1976, 117 R.I. 177, 365 A.2d 748.
288. *Procanik v. Cillo*: 1984, 97 N.J. 339, 478 A.2d 755.
289. *Raleigh Fitkin-Paul Morgan Memorial Hospital v. Anderson*: 1964, 42 N.J. 421, 201 A.2d 537 (per curiam), *cert. denied*, 377 U.S. 985.
290. *Renslow v. Mennonite Hospital*: 1977, 67 Ill.2d 348, 367 N.E.2d 1250.
291. *Reyes v. Superior Court of the State of California*: 1977, 141 Cal. Rptr. 912.
292. *Rochin v. California*: 1952, 342 U.S. 165.
293. *Roe v. Wade*: 1973, 410 U.S. 113.
294. *Roller v. Roller*: 1905, 37 Wash. 242, 79 P. 788.
295. *Schloendorff v. Society of N.Y. Hospitals*: 1914, 211 N.Y. 125, 105 N.E. 92.
296. *Schmerber v. California*: 1966, 384 U.S. 757.
297. *Smith v. Brennan*: 1960, 31 N.J. 353, 157 A.2d 497.
298. *Smyth v. Ames*: 1898, 169 U.S. 466.
299. *Snyder v. Massachusetts*: 1934, 291 U.S. 97.
300. *Stallman v. Youngquist*: 1988, No. 6457 (Ill. Sup. Ct.).
301. *State v. Allen*: 1982, 291 S.E.2d 459.
302. *State v. Richards*: 1979, 585 S.W.2d 505.
303. *Strunk v. Strunk*: 1969, 445 S.E.2d 145, 35 A.L.R.3d 683.
304. *Tarasoff v. Board of Regents of the University of California*: 1976, 17 Cal.3d 425, 551 P.2d 334, 131 Cal. Rptr. 14.
305. *Turpin v. Sortini*: 1982, 31 Cal.3d 220, 182 Cal. Rptr. 337, 643 P.2d 954.
306. *U.S. v. Crowder*: 1972, 543 F.2d 312.
307. *Webster v. Reproductive Health Services*: 1989, 109 S. Ct. 3040.
308. *Williams v. Zbaraz*: 1980, 448 U.S. 358.
309. *Winston v. Lee*: 1985, 470 U.S. 753.
310. *Womack v. Buckhorn*: 1976, 384 Mich. 718, 187 N.W.2d 218.
311. *Wright v. Olin Corp.*: 1982, 697 F.2d 1172 (4th Cir.).
312. *Zepeda v. Zepeda*: 1963, 41 Ill. App. 2d 240, 190 N.E.2d 849, *cert. denied* 1964, 379 U.S. 945.

Index

Clinical Medical Ethics

1. D. Mathieu: *Preventing Prenatal Harm.* Should the State Intervene? 1991 ISBN 0-7923-0984-7
2. N. M. P. King: *Making Sense of Advance Directives.* 1991 ISBN 0-7923-1163-9
3. E. Haavi Morreim: *Cost Balancing Act.* The New Medical Ethics of Medicine's New Economics. 1991 ISBN 0-7923-1170-1

KLUWER ACADEMIC PUBLISHERS – DORDRECHT / BOSTON / LONDON

GPSR Compliance

The European Union's (EU) General Product Safety Regulation (GPSR) is a set of rules that requires consumer products to be safe and our obligations to ensure this.

If you have any concerns about our products, you can contact us on ProductSafety@springernature.com

In case Publisher is established outside the EU, the EU authorized representative is:

Springer Nature Customer Service Center GmbH
Europaplatz 3
69115 Heidelberg, Germany

Batch number: 10824714

Printed by Printforce, the Netherlands